ELEMENTS
OF ACOUSTIC
PHONETICS

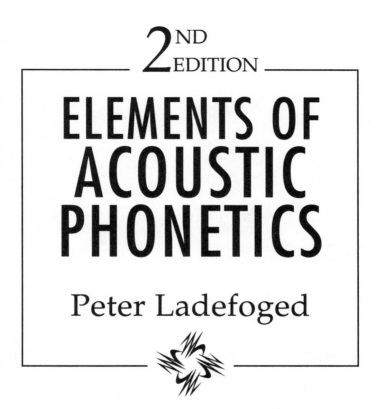

2ND EDITION

ELEMENTS OF ACOUSTIC PHONETICS

Peter Ladefoged

THE UNIVERSITY OF CHICAGO PRESS
CHICAGO AND LONDON

The University of Chicago Press, Chicago 60637
The University of Chicago Press, Ltd., London
© 1962, 1996 by Peter Ladefoged
All rights reserved. Published 1996
Printed in the United States of America

14 13 12 11 10 09 08 07 06 05   4 5 6 7 8

ISBN: 0-226-46764-3 (paper)

Library of Congress Cataloging-in-Publication Data

Ladefoged, Peter.
    Elements of acoustic phonetics / Peter Ladefoged. — 2nd ed.
        p.   cm.
    Includes bibliographical references and index.
    1. Phonetics, Acoustic.   I. Title.
    P221.5.L33   1996
    612.7'8—dc20   95-9057

CONTENTS

PREFACE

This is a new edition of *Elements of Acoustic Phonetics*, which provided, in seven short chapters, the basic aspects of acoustics that are important for the study of speech. A better title for the first edition might have been "Elements of Acoustics for Phoneticians," as it concentrated on acoustics rather than phonetics. The present book has the same general aim. The basic elements of the subject have not changed in the forty years since the earlier version was written, so the first six chapters of the book have been updated only by small changes in terminology and improved figures, drawn by special-purpose computer programs that make them more accurate. The seventh chapter has been expanded so as to take into account our modern insights into the nature of speech, and an eighth chapter added that deals with more particular phonetic issues, such as resonances of the vocal tract and how formants are related to different cavities. Additional chapters describe the really new elements that have been added to acoustic phonetics, due to the use of computers. Chapter 9 explains how computers store sound waves and some basic aspects of computer speech processing. Chapters 10 and 11 go further into computer speech processing and are inevitably a little more complicated. But without assuming any more than a vague knowledge of high school mathematics, they explain the equations used by computers in the two most common techniques for the analysis of speech sounds, Fourier analysis and Linear Predictive Coding.

The aim of the book is still to give an account of just those aspects of acoustics and digital speech processing that linguists and phoneticians need to know, without encumbering them with irrelevant material. Occasionally this has led to some oversimplification or the glossing over of points that more sophisticated readers might feel important. I have left them out so that the average speech scientist or linguist for whom this book is intended does not become daunted by too many technicalities.

I have had considerable help in refining this book from numerous students. My colleagues Pat Keating and Abeer Alwan have also made helpful comments. I am particularly indebted to Lloyd Rice, Ned Neuburg, and Tom Crystal, who taught me much of what I know about digital signal processing. They suggested good ways of presenting this material and saved me from some major infelicities. As always, I am grateful to my wife, Jenny Ladefoged, for struggling through many drafts and constantly improving the wording of every paragraph (easy reading is damned hard writing, as P. G. Wodehouse once said). With all this help, I hope the book provides a readable account of the elements of acoustic phonetics and the basic signal processing techniques used by computers for speech analysis.

CHAPTER ONE
Sound Waves

O ne of the main difficulties of studying speech is that sounds are so fleeting and transient. As each word is uttered it ceases to exist. We can, it is true, recall the sounds, either by repeating the words or by using some form of recording. But in both these cases it is another event that is happening. It is a copy of the original sound, not the sound itself.

Even during the brief existence of a sound it is curiously difficult to examine it. There is nothing that can be seen; there is no visible connecting link between a speaker and a listener. There is air around, but it is not normally possible to see any changes in the condition of the air when it is conveying a sound.

Because of these difficulties, it is perhaps best to begin our study of sound with a brief examination of the human ear. In this way we start with something tangible, for we know that the ear is the organ of hearing. Although there is still some uncertainty concerning the exact mechanism of the ear, we can nevertheless explain a number of facts about sound in terms of a simplified theory.

Figure 1.1 is a schematic diagram of the essential features of the ear. The first part to note is the eardrum,

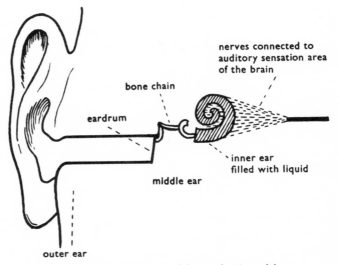

Fig. 1.1. A schematic diagram of the mechanism of the ear.

which is a thin membrane just over an inch down the narrow tube, or auditory passage, leading from the outer ear. When air is pushed down the auditory passage the eardrum tends to move with it; similarly it moves back as the air moves away. Connected to the eardrum is a chain of bones whose function is to transmit the movements of the eardrum to the liquid which is in the inner ear. Through the action of the bone chain the back-and-forth vibrations of the eardrum cause vibrations in the liquid. Closely linked with this liquid are the nerves which lead to the auditory sensation area of the brain. Movements of the liquid stimulate these nerves so that we experience the sensation of hearing. Bringing all these facts together, we may say that a sound is any disturbance of the air that could cause a displacement of the eardrum which, after transmission by the bone chain, could affect the liquid in the inner ear in such a way that the auditory nerves are stimulated. Our investigation into the nature of sound will be largely concerned with an examination of the disturbances in the air that can set off this process.

If we now turn to consider the origins of different sounds, we find that in every case some form of movement is involved. A noise occurs when a falling book hits the ground; a piano and a violin have strings that vibrate; and most speech sounds are caused by a movement of air from the lungs. It is these movements that set up the disturbances in the surrounding air.

The disturbances, however, do not occur instantaneously throughout all the air around the source of sound. They spread outward like ripples on a pond, so that there must be a short delay from the moment when the original movement caused the first disturbance to the instant when the disturbance reaches our ears. Sound travels very quickly, and consequently when we watch a person talking, we seem to hear the sounds at the same time as we see the movements that caused them. But in fact a small time has elapsed; and as we all know, in the case of a distant source of sound such as a thunderstorm, the flash of the lighting is often seen an appreciable time before the roll of thunder is heard.

In order to explain this phenomenon it is convenient to think of the air between our ears and a source of sound as being divided up into a number of particles. The source of sound causes movements of the air particles in its immediate neighborhood; these movements cause disturbances in the air a little farther away from the source; these air particles in their turn affect their neighbors which are still farther away from the source; and so the disturbance spreads outward.

We will begin our detailed examination of the production of sound by considering the note made by a tuning fork. If you look carefully at a tuning fork while it is sounding, you can see that the edges of the prongs are slightly blurred, because they are vibrating rapidly from side to side. This movement, which is shown in an exaggerated form in figure 1.2, makes a series of blows on the adjacent air. The diagram represents a moment when the

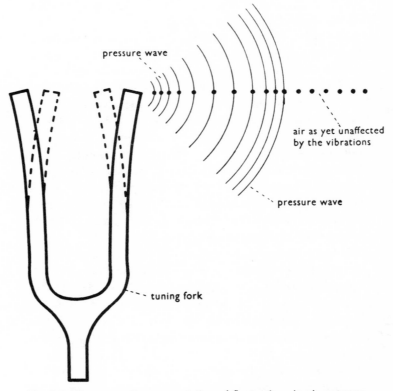

Fig. 1.2. Diagrammatic representation of fluctuations in air pressure caused by a vibrating tuning fork.

right-hand prong of the fork has moved as far as possible to the right. At that moment the particle of air immediately alongside the fork has been moved so that it is now closer to the neighboring air particles. When the air particles are close together, the air is compressed; when they are farther apart than normal, there is what is called a region of rarefaction. A moment later, as the prongs of the fork spring together again, the air will be drawn back so that there is a region of rarefaction alongside the fork.

Thus, as the fork vibrates, the air alongside it will be alternately compressed and rarefied. This disturbance of the air alongside the fork will have an effect on the particles of air a little farther away. Small displacements of the air spread outward as indicated in the diagram; when they arrive at a listener's ear they will cause the eardrum to move, and this will result in their being perceived as sound.

To get a clearer picture of the behavior of the air we may consider the motion of a limited number of particles of air. In figure 1.3, the movements of thirteen air particles are represented (in a slightly simplified form). Each line of the diagram shows their positions a short interval of time after the moment represented in the preceding line. Line six, for instance, represents the positions these thirteen particles have assumed a moment after they were in the position indicated in line five. In this diagram stationary particles are indicated by a dash; when the particle is moving an arrow is used, the speed of movement being indicated by the boldness of the arrow. Positions of the tuning fork for corresponding times are shown on the left of the figure.

It is important to note that figure 1.3 is a kind of chart, and not, like figure 1.2, a diagrammatic picture of an event. It does not represent what happens to a whole

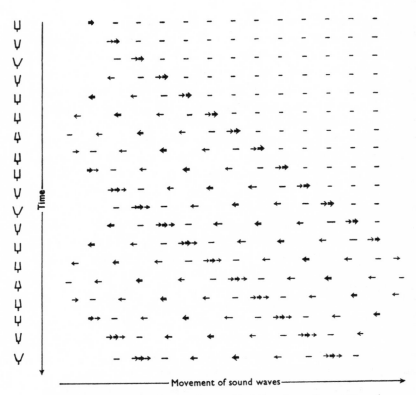

Fig. 1.3 The spreading of a sound wave. Each line shows the position of thirteen particles of air at a moment in time a little later than that in the line above. Stationary particles are indicated by a dash; moving particles are shown by arrows, the boldness of the arrow indicating the speed of movement. Highly schematized positions of a tuning fork which might have produced these movements are shown on the left. (Sophisticated readers, for whom this book is not intended, will note that the wave front has been slightly falsified in the interests of simplicity; it is assumed that the wave starts with its maximum amplitude.)

body of air when a tuning fork sounds. Only thirteen particles are represented, the successive positions of these particles being shown in successive lines. Because each line represents a moment in time later than that of the line above, the diagram should be examined one line at a time. It is a good idea to begin by placing a sheet of paper on the diagram so that only the top line is visible. As you move the paper down the page, the areas of compression and rarefaction will appear to move to the right, although the individual air particles move only backward and forward.

This kind of phenomenon is known as a wave. It is typical of a wave movement that energy in the form of areas of compression and rarefaction should be transmitted considerable distances through a medium such as the air, although the individual parts of the medium are each only slightly displaced from their positions of rest.

In order to understand exactly how a wave motion is transmitted, we must make a more detailed examination of figure 1.3. When we examine the diagram line by line we see that in the first line the prongs of the tuning fork are moving rapidly outward through their positions of rest. All the particles are stationary except the first one, which is moving in sympathy with the tuning fork. In the second line, which represents the state of affairs a moment later, the first particle is slowing down slightly, as it has pushed against the second particle, which is now moving rapidly. In the third line (a moment later still) the first particle has come to rest, and the second particle is slowing down, having set the third particle in motion. In the fourth line the third particle is still moving outward, and has even set the fourth particle in motion. The second particle, however, has stopped, and the first particle is moving back toward the tuning fork, whose prongs are now moving toward one another. Each air particle is behaving like the bob of a pendulum. If you give a pendulum a push so that it moves to one side, it will move a certain distance and then start swinging back through its position of rest; similarly, each air particle is like a pendulum which has received its push from the particle next to it. Particle seven is set in motion by particle six, which in its turn owes its movement to the push given to it by particle five, and so on.

It is in this way that vibratory motion is transmitted through the air. The individual particles move backward and forward, while the waves of compression move steadily outward. Consequently a listening ear will experience moments of higher pressure followed by moments of lower pressure. This will affect the eardrum in the way we have already mentioned, so that the sensation of sound results.

Not all variations in air pressure are perceivable as sounds. For example, we can produce by means of a fan a movement of air accompanied by a pressure wave that can be felt but not heard. In this case there is definitely a disturbance of the air; but this kind of variation in air pressure cannot be sensed by the ear, because only very rapid fluctuations of air pressure affect the ear in such a way that sounds are perceived.

Anything which causes an appropriate variation in air pressure is a source of sound. As we have seen, the changes in air pressure are due to small but frequent movements of the air particles. These have arisen because the source of sound is making similar movements. Usually the movements are far too fast to be seen with the eye. But if you put your finger lightly against a sounding tuning fork, you can often feel the vibrations. The pressure of your finger will probably stop the movement, and hence the sound will cease. In the same way you can still a ringing glass by placing a hand upon it, and thus stop the glass from vibrating. Both a glass and a tuning fork are sources of sound only as long as they are vibrating.

Another comparatively simple source of sound is a stretched string. When this is plucked or pushed to one side and then released, it springs back through and beyond its original position, and starts vibrating. This is the basis of musical instruments such as the harp, guitar, and violin. A piano also uses stretched strings, or wires, but in this case they are hit with small hammers instead of being plucked or bowed to one side. In all stretched string instruments the vibrations of the string are transferred, often through a bridge, to a sounding board of some kind, which then becomes the source of sound.

Some sources of sound do not cause such regular vibrations of the air. When a falling book hits the ground, there is a noise, although there is nothing like a stretched string or a tuning fork vibrating. The sound is caused partly by the sudden compression of the air beneath the book, and partly by the diverse irregular movements set up in both the book and the floor.

The source of sound with which we are most concerned is the human voice. Here fluctuations in air pressure are caused by a variety of means. The most important of these is the rapid opening and closing of the vocal cords. Each time the vocal folds are closed pressure is built up, which is suddenly released when they are opened. Consequently the rapid opening and closing of the folds causes a series of sharp variations in air pressure. As we shall see later (chap. 7), these variations in air pressure affect the air in the throat and mouth in such a way that speech sounds are produced.

In our discussions of sounds it will be useful to have

some means of representing them as visible shapes. This necessity leads us to a short consideration of the principles of drawing diagrams. So far we have been describing sounds in terms of the movements of the air particles, and also in terms of variations in air pressure. Our problem is to represent these movements and pressures in a suitable way. What we need is something that is sensitive to small changes in pressure or to movements of the air. A microphone is such a device in that it produces a variation in an electrical voltage that is exactly proportional to changes in the surrounding air pressure. With the aid of a microphone we can produce a graph (fig. 1.4) of the variations in air pressure which occur during the sounding of a tuning fork. In this case the changes in pressure occur at very great speeds. The pressure rises smoothly to a maximum and then falls away steadily to a minimum before rising again to repeat the cycle, all within a small fraction of a second. The height of any point on the curve above the center line represents the increase of air pressure at that time. Points below the line indicate air pressures below the normal level of the surrounding air.

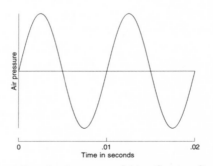

Fig. 1.4. The variations in air pressure during the sounding of a tuning fork.

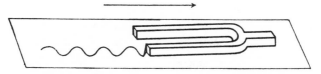

Fig. 1.5. A tuning fork being moved over a sheet of paper showing the vibrations of one of the prongs (much exaggerated).

From a diagram such as figure 1.4 we can see firstly the extent of the maximum increase of air pressure, secondly the rate at which maximum peaks of pressure occur (in this case one every one-hundredth of a second), and thirdly the way in which the pressure builds up and then decays. As these are the most important aspects of a sound wave, figure 1.4 is a useful form of diagram of a sound.

The variations in air pressure are directly related to the movements of the air particles. Peaks of pressure occur when they are close together, and moments of low pressure when they are furthest apart. Another way of representing a sound is to diagram these movements of air particles. As I stated earlier, the movement of the top of one of the prongs of a tuning fork corresponds to that of the neighboring air particles. Now it is conceptually fairly easy to make the movement of a tuning fork visible by attaching a sharp point to one prong and then drawing the vibrating fork over a sheet of paper at an even rate (fig. 1.5).

A more practical method of carrying out this experiment is to allow the vibrating fork to remain stationary above a sheet of paper wrapped round a drum which revolves at a constant speed. But in either case a curve of the form shown results.

If we now look again at figure 1.3, we can see how a

curve of a similar shape can be built up from a consideration of the movement of an air particle. In figure 1.3 the position of each particle is shown at regular intervals of time. Consequently a curve drawn through the positions of any one particle will show how much it has been displaced from its position of rest at any particular time. This is one of the most common methods of representing a sound. An example using the arrows of figure 1.3, but with the time scale shown horizontally, is given in figure 1.6. When the curve is above the line, it means that the particle, at that time, is displaced from its position of rest away from the source of sound (i.e., to the right in fig. 1.3); when the curve is below the line it means that the particle is displaced toward the source (i.e., to the left). We should also note that the particles are stationary for a brief instant at the point of their maximum displacement, and that they are moving at their fastest as they pass their original position.

Generally speaking, in this book we shall be considering sounds as variations in air pressure. Consequently the most useful form of diagram will be one which shows

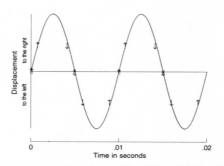

Fig. 1.6. The movement of an air particle during the sounding of a tuning fork.

how the air pressure at a given place varies over a period of time (as in fig. 1.4). We must remember, however, that it is also possible to draw a diagram of the same phenomenon by showing the movement of an individual air particle (as in fig. 1.6). These two forms of diagram are simply different ways of looking at the same event.

CHAPTER TWO
Loudness and Pitch

If you listen to a number of musical notes, such as those made by tuning forks, pianos, or violins, you will find that they may differ from one another in three principal ways. Firstly, one may be louder than another; if you strike two similar tuning forks, one gently and the other somewhat harder, almost the only difference between the two resulting sounds will be that one is soft and only just audible, whereas the other is loud and can be heard at a distance. The second possible difference between two musical sounds is that one may be higher in pitch than another. This is the main difference between two notes such as middle C and the C above it on a piano. It is possible to strike them so that they sound equally loud but differ as sounds because one is higher up the scale than the other. Lastly, the third difference between musical sounds is that one may differ in quality from another. This is the difference between two notes that are equal in pitch and loudness but have been produced by different instruments, such as a piano and a violin.

These three factors—loudness, pitch, and quality—provide the most convenient method of differentiating between all sounds. They can be regarded as three ways in which sounds can differ. Whenever you hear two sounds it is possible to describe the differences between them by comparing them in these three ways. For example, a tuning fork and an organ will produce sounds which we hear as differing in at least two of these ways. The sounds they produce may have the same pitch, but one sound is almost certain to be louder than the other, and each sound definitely has its own quality. On the other hand, when you hear the words *bed* and *bad* it is possible that they are being said on the same pitch and are equally loud. In this case they differ in only one respect, that of quality. One of the main purposes of this book is to provide a way of talking about sounds so that it is possible to give a physical description of the variations in air pressure corresponding to these differences. For the remainder of this chapter we shall examine the two simpler differences—those of loudness and pitch—and see if we can discover the different conditions of the air corresponding to each of them.

It is quite easy to see how it is that sounds differ in loudness. If you strike a tuning fork hard the prongs begin by making large vibrations which, as the sound dies away, gradually become smaller and smaller. Similarly you produce a loud noise by plucking a string hard or striking the notes on a piano forcibly. So it is reasonable to assume that a large movement of the source of sound produces a loud sound, and that a small movement results in a soft sound. If we consider this from the point of view of the vibrations of the air, we see that a large movement of the source produces a large movement of the air particles. Or considering a sound as consisting of fluctuations in air pressure, a large movement of the source causes great fluctuations of air pressure. From the listener's point of view, these large fluctuations of air pressure cause a correspondingly large movement of the eardrum and are interpreted as loud sounds.

Our method of diagramming sounds is to show how the air pressure increases and decreases. We can now see how to diagram a difference of loudness between two sounds. Figure 2.1 is a diagram of two sounds, one being a loud sound, where the variations in air pressure are large, and the other a soft sound, where they are much smaller. Figure 2.2 is a diagram (somewhat exaggerated) of the variations in pressure accompanying a tuning fork which has been struck fairly hard and then allowed to come to rest. Immediately after the fork has been struck, the resulting variations in air pressure become gradually less and less.

The extent of the maximum variation in air pressure from normal during a sound is called the *amplitude* of that sound. In figure 2.1 the lines a–a' and b–b' represent the amplitudes of the two sounds. As you can see, in this case one is about twice the other. Because the one amplitude is larger than the other, the one sound is louder than the other. But owing to the nature of sound and the

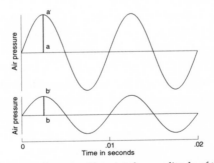

Fig. 2.1. Two sounds, one with twice the amplitude of the other.

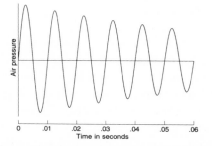

Fig. 2.2. A diagram (somewhat exaggerated) of part of the sound produced by a tuning fork which has been struck and is gradually coming to rest.

structure of our ears, we do not consider the one sound to be twice as loud as the other. Chapter 6 will give a more specific account of the relation between amplitude and loudness. For the moment all we need to note is that if the amplitude of a sound decreases (i.e., if the peaks of pressure during the sound become weaker), then the sound becomes less loud.

The human ear is very sensitive to differences in air pressure. For the softest sound we can hear, the air pressure alongside our eardrum has to vary by only one part in 10,000,000,000; but for the loudest sounds that we can stand without a feeling of pain in our ears, the pressure may be varying by more than a million times that amount.

The differences in the condition of the air corresponding to loud and soft sounds are much as we might expect. We know that we have to put more energy into making a loud noise than into making a soft one. It is hardly surprising that in a loud noise there is a bigger disturbance being transmitted through the air, and consequently a greater movement of our eardrums. There is, however, one point to be careful about: in order to build up a larger variation in air pressure, the particles move farther and more rapidly. But this does not mean that the peaks of pressure must occur more frequently. As you can see in figure 2.1, although one sound has twice the amplitude of the other, the peaks of pressure in both of them are still occurring at the same rate of one every one-hundredth of a second. One of the two tuning forks may be making larger vibrations than the other, but they are both making the same number of complete vibrations per second.

In order to make this point quite clear, it is worth while conducting a simple experiment. If you make two pendulums, each consisting of about a yard of string with a weight tied on one end, they will both take about two seconds to make a complete swing. Now if you start one pendulum by pulling it only slightly to one side, and the other by pulling it much farther to one side, the one will be making vibrations of small amplitude, and the other vibrations of large amplitude. But they will nevertheless both be making about the same number of swings in a minute. If one is making fewer vibrations per minute than the other (because the string is longer), it will always vibrate that way no matter how hard you push it. The time taken for a complete swing (of a pendulum or of a tuning fork) does not depend on the amplitude or size of each swing.

If we do vary the rate at which a tuning fork is vibrating, then we vary the rate at which peaks of pressure occur (as opposed to the strength of each peak, which is the amplitude). When we do this, we find that we are causing differences between sounds in one of the other ways, namely, that of pitch. The difference between a tuning fork of high pitch and one of low pitch is that the higher-pitched one is making a greater number of vibrations per second. Consequently a diagram of a high note as compared with a low note is as shown in figure 2.3. Both sounds have peaks of pressure of the same amplitude; but as you can see from the time scale, in the one they are occurring every 1/100 of a second, whereas in the other they occur more frequently, namely, every 1/300 of a second.

The variations in air pressure in any sound that has a definite pitch must form a pattern which is repeated at regular intervals of time. In the case of the tuning forks which we have been discussing, the pattern consists of an increase to a peak of pressure, followed by a decrease to a minimum before again rising to normal. A complete variation in air pressure of this sort is called a cycle. Thus a cycle is the variation in pressure from the moment when the pressure changes in a certain manner, to the next moment when it changes in precisely the same way and starts to go through the same pattern of changes again. A cycle occurs every 1/100 of a second for the first sound in figure 2.3, and every 1/300 of a second for the

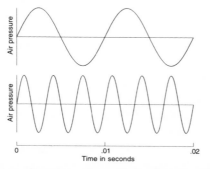

Fig. 2.3. Two sounds with equal amplitudes, but one with peaks of air pressure occurring every one-hundredth of a second and the other with three peaks occurring within one-hundredth of a second.

other sound. Therefore there must be in the first case 100 cycles per second, and in the second case 300 cycles per second. This rate at which cycles occur is known as the frequency, and is measured in hertz (usually abbreviated to Hz). The two sounds in question have frequencies of 100 Hz and 300 Hz. For most practical purposes we can say that the pitch depends on the frequency or rate of repetition of the variations in air pressure. The second sound in figure 2.3 has a higher pitch than the first because it has a higher frequency—i.e., during the second sound there is a greater number of complete variations in air pressure (complete cycles) in one second than there is during the first sound.

In order to understand the difference between frequency and amplitude it is seriously suggested that you perform the experiment with the two pendulums, as described above. You will then discover that a given pendulum will vibrate with varying amplitude but with a constant frequency. It will always take the same length of time to make one swing backward and forward (i.e., one cycle), irrespective of the size of the swing. The corresponding acoustic fact is that a given tuning fork may produce relatively large or small peaks of pressure, but each complete variation in air pressure will have the same duration. Thus the cycle of variations in air pressure will always be repeated the same number of times each second; or in other words, the frequency of the sound will always be the same. Putting this in our everyday language, we can say that the sounds produced by a given tuning fork will all have the same pitch, although they may vary in loudness. Only by altering the length of the pendulum or the size of the tuning fork can we alter the duration of each cycle, and so vary the frequency.

Whenever a definite pitch can be assigned to a sound,

the air is being made to vibrate in a regular manner. For example, when a tuning fork of a standard pitch A is struck, compressions and rarefactions occur in the surrounding air at a rate of 440 a second; each wave of compression follows exactly 1/440 of a second after the preceding one. Consequently, if our eardrums are affected by such a sound, they move backward and forward 440 times in a second.

Sounds with a low pitch have a low frequency; accordingly, many of the sources of sound that produce low notes are large and heavy things which vibrate slowly. Just as a long pendulum vibrates more slowly than a short one, so a large bell has a lower frequency of vibration—consequently producing a lower note—than a small bell. Similarly the long heavy strings of a piano are at the bass, while the higher-frequency notes at the treble end are produced by smaller strings. Sometimes when listening to the very low notes of an organ, you get the impression that you can feel, and can almost count, the separate peaks of air pressure. This kind of sensation never occurs when you are listening to a high note.

When a note is exactly twice the frequency of another note, it is said to be an octave higher. Thus standard pitch A on a piano is 440 Hz; the A above it (often written a') is 880 Hz; and A above that (a″) is 1,760 Hz. Remember that these figures correspond to the frequency of occurrence of the cycles of air pressure. These will occur at a rate similar to the frequency of vibration of the source of the sound, and the frequency of vibration of our eardrums. The lowest frequency which our ears can detect as a sound is about 16–20 Hz. The highest frequency we can hear is about 20,000 Hz; above that frequency we cannot detect sounds, probably because our eardrums and the chain of connecting bones cannot vibrate fast enough.

When studying speech, however, we are primarily concerned with frequencies far below this. The fastest vibration an ordinary telephone can transmit is about 3,500 Hz. Most of the frequencies of interest in the analysis of speech are below 8,000 Hz.

The frequency of a note can be varied in different ways. As we have noted, other things being equal, a tuning fork with long prongs vibrates more slowly (i.e., produces a note of lower frequency) than a fork with short prongs. Similarly a long stretched string, as on a double bass, vibrates more slowly than the shorter string on a violin, which is consequently higher in pitch. Another way of altering the frequency of a string is to increase the tension. Thus a violinist tuning his instrument tightens or loosens the strings so as to raise or lower the frequency. The vocal cords, which I will discuss later, vibrate more rapidly when they are under greater tension. Finally, variation in the mass of a vibrating body will affect the frequency. A heavy string of a given length and under a certain tension will vibrate more slowly than an equally taut light string of the same length. The heavier vocal folds of men generally produce a lower pitch than women's vocal cords, which are usually smaller and lighter.

We use the word *pitch* when we are referring to that aspect of a sound whereby we can, using only our ears, place it on a scale going from low to high. When we are discussing actual rates of vibration or rates of fluctuations in air pressure, we speak of the frequency of the sound. Similarly, loudness is the term we use when we are describing one of the ways in which we can hear sounds differ. It corresponds (more or less) to the instrumentally measurable factor which we call the intensity of the sound. The intensity is derivable from the amplitude or amount of increase in pressure during a sound. In chapter 6 I shall expand and qualify these remarks. But for the moment we can take it that when only the frequency of a sound is altered, then only the pitch is varied. Similarly, when the amplitude of a sound is increased while the frequency remains unaltered, then we hear an increase in loudness.

CHAPTER THREE
Quality

In the last chapter we saw how variations in pitch and loudness occur. Now we must consider differences in quality. We must try to explain, for instance, the differences between middle C played on a piano and on a violin; or, what is more important for phoneticians, how it is possible to make different vowel sounds on the same pitch.

So far we have considered in detail only one type of musical note—that produced by a tuning fork. The back-and-forth movements of the prongs of a tuning fork are steady and regular. As we saw in chapter 1, a point attached to the prong of a sounding tuning fork will draw a smooth curve as it is moved over a sheet of paper. The technical name for a mathematically specified wave very similar to this is a *sine wave*. In chapter 10 I will give a more detailed account of the nature of sine waves.

Not all sounds have such simple wave forms as those produced by tuning forks. This is because most sources of sound vibrate in a far more complex way. Figure 3.1 shows the wave shape that occurs when a note on a piano is played. Remember that this diagram means that if we could measure the air pressure we would find that it went up and down in the way shown. If you were listen-

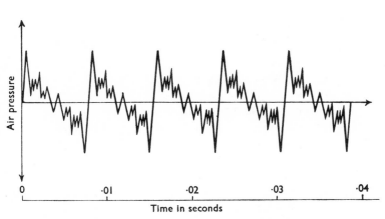

Fig. 3.1. The waveform of the C below middle C on a piano.

ing to this note the air pressure alongside your eardrum would waver up and down as indicated in figure 3.1. A microphone used in conjunction with other equipment can record these changes in air pressure. This diagram is based on a record of air-pressure measurements made with the aid of a microphone placed a short distance away from a piano.

When there are such complex fluctuations of pressure the particles of air must be moving in a complicated way. Particles of air agitated by the vibrations of a tuning fork move merely backward and forward in the simple way I have already described. Their motion corresponded to that of the bob of a pendulum; from their maximum position of displacement they started slowly, gradually increasing their speed until they reached their normal position, and from there on slowing down until they reached their maximum displacement in the other direction. As we have seen, this kind of movement corresponds to fluctuations in air pressure which can be represented by means of the smooth curves known as sine waves.

The variations in air pressure that occur when a vowel is spoken are far more complex. In other words, the movements of the air particles conveying such a sound are very complex. And this, in turn, is due to the complex way in which the air in the vocal tract vibrates. Unlike the prongs of a tuning fork, which simply move backward and forward, this body of air can be made to vibrate in several ways at once. The notion of a body vibrating in several ways simultaneously is illustrated in figure 3.2, which shows how different parts of a string can be vibrating in different ways at the same time. A piano string and the piano soundboard vibrate in a complex way such as this, and consequently cause the complex variations in air pressure which are represented in figure 3.1.

If you look at figure 3.1 you will see that the variations in air pressure have a certain regularity. Once every 1/100 of a second, the whole complex pattern repeats itself. As I said earlier, a pattern of variations in air pressure which is repeated at regular intervals of time is known as a cycle; and the pitch of a sound is dependent largely on the rate at which the cycles recur. In the particular waveform which we are considering, the rate of repetition of the cycles—the frequency—is 100 cycles per second, or 100 Hz. If this frequency were increased, the pitch would be

Fig. 3.2. Solid line: one position of a vibrating string. Dashed line: another position, giving an impression of vibration of parts of the string. Taken as a whole, the string may be said to vibrate in many ways at the same time.

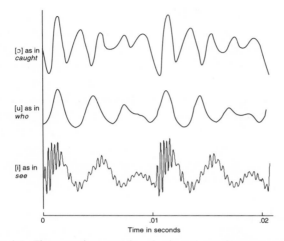

Fig. 3.3. The waveform produced when the author pronounced the vowels [ɔ] as in *caught*, [u] as in *who*, and [i] as in *see* at a fundamental frequency of approximately 100 Hz. In this and all the following figures unless otherwise noted, the vertical scale represents variations in air pressure.

raised; conversely, if the frequency were decreased, the pitch would become lower. Nearly all the diagrams of sound waves in this book include a time scale. Accordingly it is usually possible to calculate the fundamental frequency of repetition of the sound waves. You should check that when the text refers to, e.g., a 100 Hz wave, the diagram shows a wave form which repeats itself every 0.01 second as indicated by the time scale.

The difference between the qualities of the sounds of a tuning fork, a piano, and a vowel is due to the difference in the complexity of the waveform. Whenever sounds differ in quality we find that they have different wave shapes. Figure 3.3 shows the wave shapes produced when the author said three vowels, [ɔ] as in *caught*, [u] as in *who,* and [i] as in *see.* (The phonetic symbols used in this book are those of the International Phonetic Association's alphabet.) These waves have very complex shapes, but you can see that the vowels were all pronounced on the same pitch; in each of them the complex pattern repeats itself every one-hundredth of a second. The differences between these vowel sounds are all in the quality dimension. They are heard as different vowels because each has a characteristic wave shape; but they are heard as being on the same pitch because the complex waveform of each of them is repeated at the same rate.

One of the main objects of this book is to build up a way of describing sound waves. We have seen how to specify the pitch in terms of the frequency, or number of vibrations per second, and the loudness in terms of the amplitude, or magnitude of the pressure changes. We now have to try to describe quality in terms of the complex wave shapes.

The frequency of all these vowels is approximately 100 Hz, since the main pattern repeats itself about once every one-hundredth of a second. But in each vowel we can see one or two other more or less regular waves superimposed on top of the main pattern. In the vowel [ɔ] as in *caught,* this added wave repeats itself about five times for every single repetition of the main pattern (you can count five peaks within each repetition). We know that the frequency of repetition of the complex wave is 100 Hz. So the smaller wave in [ɔ] has a frequency of around 500 Hz. Similarly in the vowel [u] as in *who,* there is a wave whose frequency is a little over three times that of the fundamental frequency, as there are three peaks within each repetition; consequently it is approximately 300 Hz. The vowel [i] as in *see,* on the other hand, has two waves which can be separated out by eye. One has a frequency of about 250 Hz, since it repeats itself nearly two and a half times during each repetition of the complex pattern. The other is a wave representing a far more rapid variation in air pressure. It looks as if it were superimposed on top of the 250 Hz wave, and occurs about 27 times during each repetition of the complex pattern (you can count about 27 small peaks). The frequency of this wave is therefore about 2,700 Hz.

We can now see how differences in quality may be described. The vowels [i] *see*, [ɔ] *caught*, and [u] *who*, when they are all said on the same pitch (100 Hz), are characterized by the presence of additional frequencies; the approximate values of the principal extra frequencies are 500 Hz for [ɔ], 300 Hz for [u], and 250 Hz and 2,700 Hz for [i]. This is, of course, a gross oversimplification of the situation. As we shall see later, complex sounds like vowels actually have to be described as consisting of far more than two or three frequencies, and the values given for the vowels in this particular figure are not appropriate descriptions of these vowels in general. But this method of analysis by visual inspection provides a useful basis for a preliminary description.

If we now try to synthesize these vowels by sounding a number of pure tones simultaneously, we can see the failings in this form of analysis. Let us suppose we try to synthesize the vowel [ɔ] as in *caught* by sounding a fairly loud tuning fork of 100 Hz (because this was the basic frequency of repetition of the complex wave shape), plus an additional tuning fork with a frequency of 500 Hz (because this was the main superimposed frequency that was characteristic of this vowel). Figure 3.4 is a diagram of the variations in air pressure that result when these two forks are sounded separately. When they are sounded together the air pressure is affected by both of them. Figure

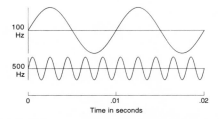

Fig. 3.4. The variations in air pressure which result when two tuning forks, one with a frequency of 100 Hz and the other with a frequency of 500 Hz, are sounded separately.

3.5 is a diagram of this situation. The thinner lines represent the pressure variations that would be produced by the individual forks, and the darker line represents the composite waveform that results from combining these waves. As you can see, when both forks are working together to increase the pressure (as at the times marked *a*), the resultant pressure is above that produced by either alone; similarly, when both forks are working together to decrease the pressure, the resulting pressure is less than that which would result from the action of either fork alone; but when the two forks are working against each other, one trying to increase the pressure while the other is trying to decrease it (as at the times marked *b*), the resultant pressure is somewhere between the two.

The wave shape in figure 3.5, however, is not very similar to the wave shape of the vowel [ɔ] in figure 3.3. But this is hardly surprising, since two tuning forks sounded together do not sound like a vowel. These two wave shapes, which may represent variations in air pressure alongside our ears (and consequently are directly related to the movements of our eardrums), are not the wave shapes of identical sounds. The wave shape of any vowel is far more complex than that of two tuning forks.

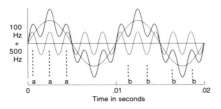

Fig. 3.5. The complex wave which results when the two waves shown in fig. 3.4 are superimposed.

In our study of the acoustics of speech sounds we shall have to consider wave shapes that are even more complex than those of vowels. Figure 3.6 is a diagram of the sound wave that occurs during the [s] at the end of the word *mouse*. We can, as usual, take it as a representation of the changes in air pressure which occur alongside our eardrums. These changes will, of course, cause movements of the eardrum which will be perceived by the brain as sounds. But unlike all the other sounds we have considered so far, the movements of the eardrum will be irregular, since the air pressure goes up and down in an irregular manner.

It is often convenient to consider sounds in which the variations in air pressure do not follow a regular pattern as being in a different class from those in which there is a cycle of variation in air pressure which is exactly repeated at regular intervals of time. Figure 3.7 is a diagram of another sound with a nonrepetitive wave form. Note especially that although the variations in air pressure that occur during the period from time *a* to time *b* are similar to those which occur during the period from time *b* to time *c*, their amplitude is distinctly greater, and therefore they are not identical. In this sound there is no pattern of variations in air pressure which is exactly repeated at regular intervals of time.

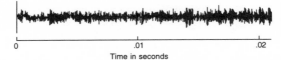

Time in seconds

Fig. 3.6. Part of the sound wave that occurred during the pronunciation
of the [s] at the end of the word *mouse*.

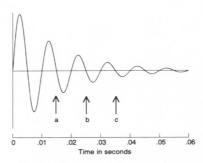

Time in seconds

Fig. 3.7. A nonrepetitive waveform.

Of course, if we are being precise in our discussion of
sounds, we must admit that every sound we have discussed so far (and, indeed, every sound we are ever
likely to discuss) has in fact a nonrepetitive wave form. In
no real sound is there a pattern of variations in air pressure which is repeated exactly at regular intervals of time
for ever and ever. As we have seen, even the vibrations of
a tuning fork die away eventually; consequently each
wave has a little less amplitude and is not precisely the
same as the wave that preceded it. Moreover, the fork is
set in motion by a blow; until a steady state of vibration
has been reached, the waves are far from exactly repetitive. However, the errors resulting from disregarding
these factors are very small. We shall, as a matter of con-

venience, consider some sounds to have cycles of variations in air pressure that are repeated exactly at regular intervals of time, whereas other sounds we shall consider to have nonrepetitive waveforms. (The distinction between these two classes of sounds is considered further in chapter 7.)

Both classes of sounds are of great interest to students of speech. As we know, spoken words consist of sounds which are continually changing in quality. Sometimes, as at the beginning and end of the word *peak,* the waveform is altering very rapidly. The variations in air pressure which affect our ears are very sudden and irregular; consequently we shall consider the word *peak* to begin and end with a nonrepetitive waveform. In comparison with such sounds, the middle part of the word *peak* lasts for an appreciable length of time without much alteration in quality; we shall therefore consider this part of the word to consist of regular variations in air pressure.

One of the characteristics of sounds with nonrepetitive waveforms is that they cannot be said to have any precise pitch. As we saw earlier, the pitch of a sound is largely dependent on the frequency with which the cycle of variations in air pressure is repeated. Sounds in which no part of the waveform is exactly and constantly repeated do not have any definite pitch. When we listen to the irregular variations in air pressure caused by the striking of a match or the rustling of leaves, we find that we can say very little about the pitch of these sounds. Nor do the nonrepetitive waveforms at the beginning and end of the word *peak* produce any precise sensations of pitch. If this word can be said to have been spoken on a definite pitch, it is due to the more regular variations in air pressure which occur in the middle part of the word.

One of the main differences between this book and

general books on acoustics is that we are often concerned with nonrepetitive waveforms. We shall have to deal with all sorts of sounds, varying from those which have virtually no pattern at all in their waveform to those where the waveform is almost, but not quite, exactly repetitive. There is a special name for the sound with the most complex nonrepetitive wave form. It is called *white noise*. The name is due to the analogy of white light, which is light that is made up of all the colors of the rainbow. White noise is a complex sound composed of equal amounts of all audible tones. The nearest approach to it with which we are all familiar is the background hiss which occurs on a radio.

Several sounds occur in speech which are almost as complex as white noise. We have already mentioned the sound that occurs at the end of the word *mouse*. Other sounds of this sort occur at the beginning and end of the word *fish*.

A somewhat less complex waveform, which is also of great interest to us in our study of speech, was illustrated in figure 3.7. This is the sort of sound that occurs when a body of air such as that in the vocal tract is given a sharp tap. The diagram indicates that the air pressure varies in a fairly regular way, but the amplitude of each peak of pressure is considerably less than the amplitude of the preceding peak of pressure.

Finally, we must consider here the sound corresponding to a very sharp tap on some object which has no tendency to vibrate. If the tap were sharp enough, it could theoretically cause the air pressure to rise instantaneously and then to fall away again equally rapidly, as shown in figure 3.8. A pressure change this sharp has some interesting theoretical properties which we will discuss later, but it could never really happen. The nearest

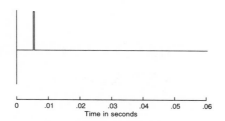

Fig. 3.8 The sound wave of a very sharp tap or click.

approach to this sort of sound is the click that occurs when we switch a loudspeaker on or off.

As we shall see further in the next chapter, the division of all sounds into two classes, depending on whether they can be considered to have a nonrepetitive waveform or not, is made for convenience in analysis. It would be useful if there were a general term which could be used to describe all sounds with nonrepetitive waveforms, including a hissing noise which goes on for some considerable time, a dull thud which occurs when a falling object hits the ground, and a click which is the result of a single sharp variation in air pressure. As there is no accepted generic term for all these sounds, however, we shall have to continue to describe them as sounds which can be considered to have nonrepetitive waveforms—a somewhat cumbersome phrase, but one that cannot be avoided.

CHAPTER FOUR
Wave Analysis

We saw in the last chapter that two pure tones can combine to produce a complex wave shape. What is not so easy to see is that any waveform whatsoever can be synthesized from a sufficient number of pure tones. The waveforms of the vowels in figure 3.3 and the non-repetitive waveforms which we discussed at the end of the last chapter can all be synthesized, provided we take enough pure tones and combine them in an appropriate manner.

The method of analysis in which a complex wave is regarded as a suitable combination of a number of pure tones is known as Fourier analysis. The theorem underlying it was discovered by the French mathematician Fourier in 1822. It is such a basic concept in acoustics that it is worthwhile considering a number of illustrations.

We may start by combining a 100 Hz wave with a small 200 Hz wave and a somewhat larger 300 Hz wave. The result is shown in figure 4.1. The complex wave is simply the result of adding the increases in air pressure (i.e., those points on the curve above the line representing normal pressure) and subtracting the decreases in air pressure (those points below the line). At time x, for instance, two of the pure tones were causing increases in

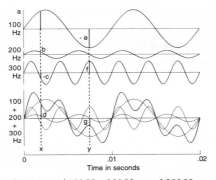

Fig. 4.1. A combination of 100 Hz, 200 Hz, and 300 Hz waves forming a complex wave.

pressure of amounts represented by the lines *a* and *b*, whereas the third was causing a decrease in pressure of amount represented by the line *c*. The resultant air pressure has an amplitude represented by the line *d*, whose length is equivalent to *a* + *b* − *c*. Similarly, at time *y* the resultant air pressure is −*g* (minus because it is below the line; i.e., the point represents a moment of rarefaction or decrease in pressure). In this case −*g* = *e* + *f*. The 200 Hz component has no effect at this moment, as its amplitude is zero. Any point in the complex wave can be treated in this way. The pressure at that instance is always the result of combining (adding or subtracting) the pressure changes that would have been caused by the individual component waves. In order to verify this, try measuring the heights of the component waves at any appropriate time and check that they do combine to produce the point which occurs at the same instant on the complex wave.

If we had intercepted a complex wave such as we have synthesized in figure 4.1, our problem would be to know how to describe it. First of all, we can see that the frequency of repetition of the complex waveform is 100 Hz. This is known as the *fundamental frequency,* or sometimes just as the *fundamental.* The pitch that we hear depends primarily on the fundamental frequency.

In order to describe the waveform more fully, we have to state the components of the complex wave. In this case we can say that it can be considered as being composed of a fundamental frequency of 100 Hz plus two other tones. These additional tones are known as *harmonics.* A harmonic is any whole-number multiple of the fundamental frequency. In the wave we are considering, the components are called the second and third harmonics, because one is twice, and the other is three times, the fundamental frequency. If there had been components of 400 Hz and 1,000 Hz, they would have been called the fourth and tenth harmonics.

In some of the older textbooks on acoustics, the component with a frequency twice that of the fundamental is called the first harmonic, and the component with a frequency three times that of the fundamental is called the second harmonic, etc. We reject this old habit because its arithmetic is confusing, like the French "eight days" for "a week," and "fifteen days" for "a fortnight." In this book the second harmonic will always have a frequency which is twice that of the fundamental.

A more complete specification of the waveform in figure 4.1 would state not only the frequencies of the components (in this case 100 Hz, 200 Hz, and 300 Hz) but also their amplitudes (i.e., the size of the peaks of pressure in these components). As we have drawn it, the fundamental frequency is the largest of the three, the second harmonic is considerably smaller, and the third is about three-fifths the size of the fundamental. If we represented the relative amplitudes of the components by the relative lengths of lines, we could draw a diagram as shown in figure 4.2. This kind of diagram is of considerable importance in acoustics. It is called the *spectrum* of a sound. It is a statement of the components of a sound and thus provides a simpler description than is given by a diagram of the complex wave shape.

It is possible to draw a diagram of the spectrum of any sound. For instance, when we were trying to synthesize the vowel [ɔ] as in *caught* by sounding two tuning forks (fig. 3.5), we could have drawn a diagram of the situation in the form shown in figure 4.3. The complex wave we

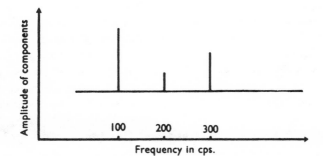

Fig. 4.2. The spectrum of the complex wave illustrated in fig. 4.1.

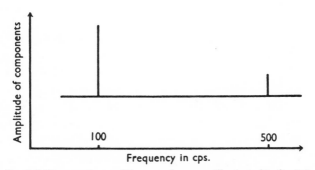

Fig. 4.3. The spectrum of the complex wave illustrated in fig. 3.5.

produced had two components, one being a 100 Hz wave
(the fundamental) and the other being a 500 Hz wave (the
fifth harmonic of the fundamental). The relative amplitudes of the components were 3 to 1, i.e., the fundamental was much more powerful than the harmonic. All this
information is conveyed by the diagram in figure 4.3.
Similarly we could draw a diagram of the components of
the complex wave produced by a piano. The C below
middle C, whose waveform was illustrated in figure 3.1,
can be described in terms of the spectrum shown in figure 4.4. This shows that the complex wave may be considered as being composed of a fundamental and a large
number of harmonics. Apart from the fifteenth and six-
teenth harmonics, which are missing or too faint to show
up, all the harmonics up to the eighteenth play a part in
building up the complex wave. Note that in these diagrams only the frequency scale is calibrated. No absolute
values for the amplitudes are marked, because the shape
of the complex wave is determined by the relative
strength of the components. When the amplitude of a
complex wave is increased (i.e., when the sound be-

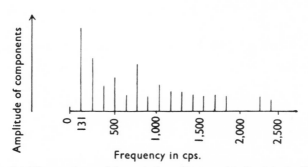

Fig. 4.4. The spectrum of the waveform illustrated in fig. 3.1, the C below middle C on a piano.

comes louder), the amplitudes of all the components are increased in the same proportion.

A diagram of the spectrum of a sound does leave out some of the information that is present in the complex wave. In some senses it is a simplification, since it does not tell us everything about the way in which the components are combined. In figure 4.1 the components were drawn so that at the point at which the diagram starts the component waves were all about to cause an increase in pressure. But now suppose that these pure tones (which may represent sounds accompanying tuning forks) were not combined in this way. If we are thinking in terms of a wave that we have synthesized, it is quite conceivable that one tuning fork should have been started before the others. Consequently, at the time when they were brought close together (which may be thought of as time zero on the diagram), the situation might be as in figure 4.5. Here, at the start of the diagram, the tuning fork with the lowest frequency is about to cause an increase in pressure, the second tuning fork is producing a wave which is about to decline from a peak of maximum pressure, and the third tuning fork is about to cause a decrease in pressure. If we now combine the pressure variations, as we did on the previous occasions, the resulting complex wave is as shown. At any moment the pressure of the complex wave is the result of adding or subtracting the pressure of the components. For example, at the times marked *a* and *b* the variation from normal air pressure is zero, because at these points the pressure changes caused by the components cancel out.

This complex waveform repeats itself one hundred times a second. In this respect it is the same as the wave in figure 4.1, but in other ways these waves look very different. Yet each of them has components with the same fre-

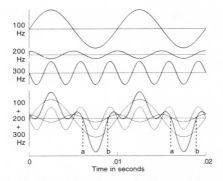

Fig. 4.5. A combination of 100 Hz, 200 Hz, and 300 Hz waves, differing from the combination in fig. 4.1 with respect to their relative timing, and consequently forming a different complex wave.

quencies and amplitudes. The difference is due solely to the way in which these components are combined. This difference in the timing of the components is known as a difference of phase.

Because the waves in figures 4.1 and 4.5 can be analyzed into the same components, the diagrams of their spectra will be the same. The spectrum of a sound shows only which frequencies are present and with what amplitudes; it does not usually specify the way in which the components are combined. Figure 4.2 is therefore the spectrum corresponding to both the wave in figure 4.1 and that in figure 4.5, as it designates a sound with a fundamental of 100 Hz combined with a second harmonic with 3/10 of the amplitude of the fundamental and a third harmonic with 3/5 of the amplitude of the fundamental.

It is possible to produce pure tones which may be combined so as to make either of the waveforms corresponding to the spectrum shown in figure 4.2. These illustrations were produced by a computer that could have been producing sounds just as easily as graphical illustrations. It is even possible to alter the way in which the pure tones are combined, so that the waveform of figure 4.1 changes slowly into that of figure 4.5, passing through a variety of other waveforms on the way. The astonishing thing is that our ears can hear no difference between all these waveforms. As long as the components stay the same, the sound will be the same. Apart from special cases involving very loud sounds (which are probably irrelevant as far as the acoustics of speech is concerned), the quality of a sound does not depend on the way in which the components are combined; it depends simply on the frequencies and the amplitudes of the component waves.

We can now see why it is that the waveform does not provide a satisfactory method of describing the quality of a sound. We may consider two sounds to be identical because they have the same components; but they may nevertheless have very different waveforms. Moreover, it is possible for any sound (e.g., the vowel [i] as in *see*) to have one waveform on one occasion and to have a different waveform on another occasion. We should hear both sounds as being the same vowel, provided the components of these different waves were the same. Consequently it is often better to represent a sound by a diagram showing its spectrum rather than by a diagram of its wave form. The spectrum of the vowel [i] as in *see* will always be the same as long as the components are the same.

So far all our analyses have been of sounds with a definite frequency. But it is also possible to specify the spectra of sounds with nonrepetitive waveforms, such as that shown in figure 4.6. This wave can be analyzed into a number of pure tones (which are, of course, regular waves) in much the same way as the repetitive wave-

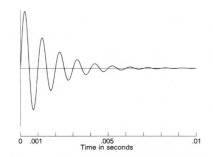

0   .001   .005   .01
                       Time in seconds

Fig. 4.6. A nonrepetitive waveform in which peaks of pressure occur at the rate of 1,000 per second for as long as the sound lasts.

forms which we have been considering in this chapter up until now. If we examine the waveform in figure 4.6, we can see that, while the sound lasts, peaks of pressure occur every one-thousandth of a second. Consequently we may well expect to find that one component of this sound has a frequency of 1,000 Hz. All we have to find in addition are some components which will cause the amplitude of the complex wave to become less and less.

It turns out that if we add to the 1,000 Hz wave one component with a slightly lower frequency and another with a slightly higher frequency, we achieve something like the result we desire. These two waves, along with the 1,000 Hz wave, are shown in the upper part of figure 4.7. One of them has a frequency of 900 Hz and the other a frequency of 1,100 Hz; both have amplitudes half as large as the 1,000 Hz wave. The result of combining these three waves for a limited time is shown in the lower part of figure 4.7.

As you can see in the figure, at time *a* both these waves are assisting the 1,000 Hz component to increase the pressure; consequently the first peak of pressure is fairly

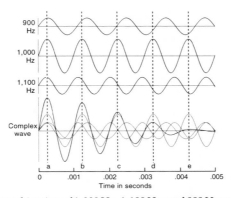

Fig. 4.7. A combination of 1,000 Hz, 1,100 Hz, and 900 Hz waves to form a complex wave.

large. At time *b*, they are both assisting, but not so much, so that the second peak is somewhat smaller. At time *c* they almost cancel each other out, their combined effect being to cause only a slight increase in the peak of pressure due to the 1,000 Hz wave alone. At time *d* they are causing a small decrease in the maximum pressure. This effect is enhanced at time *e*, when they are causing a considerable lowering in the peak of pressure. These three waves therefore can be combined for a short period to produce a wave shape similar to the waveform we wished to analyze.

As the complex wave shown in figure 4.7 looks very like the complex wave in figure 4.6 it might seem that we could describe this wave form as having a spectrum similar to that shown in figure 4.8, i.e., as being composed of pure tones with frequencies of 900 Hz, 1,000 Hz, and 1,100 Hz, the 900 Hz and 1,100 Hz tones each having an amplitude half that of the 1,000 Hz tone. However, this is not quite true, as the complex wave in figure 4.7 is not

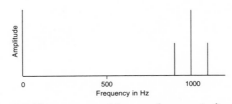

Fig. 4.8. The spectrum of the complex wave in fig. 4.7.

exactly the same as the wave in figure 4.6. The latter sound started abruptly, presumably from silence, and then faded away, presumably into silence again. But the component waves which have to be added together to make the complex wave in figure 4.7 are all pure tones: i.e., in each wave, each cycle is the same as the following one, which is the same as the next one, and so on, theoretically to infinity. But if the pure tones indicated in figure 4.7 were combined for a longer period, they would go on to produce a waveform as shown in figure 4.9. The wave in figure 4.6 was roughly the same as that part of the complex wave between the dotted lines. Consequently we see that it would be only an approximation to the truth to say that this waveform had the spectrum shown in figure 4.8. An analysis of this waveform into the three components shown in the spectrum makes no pretense at taking into account the fact that the sound which we set out to analyze had a sudden beginning and was followed by silence.

If we do make allowances for the silence that preceded and followed the wave in figure 4.6, we find that we have to analyze the waveform into a large (actually an infinite) number of components. Naturally we cannot demonstrate this by diagramming all these components. But by representing some of them we can indicate the shape of the spectrum they would produce (fig. 4.10). The more

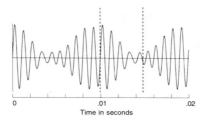

Fig. 4.9. A complex wave (with a fundamental frequency of 100 Hz) composed of three waves with frequencies of 900, 1,000, and 1,100 Hz. Fig. 4.7 showed only that part of this wave which is between the dashed lines.

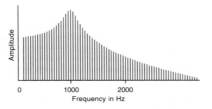

Fig. 4.10. A close approximation to the spectrum of the sound wave shown in fig. 4.6.

usual method of diagramming these components is by means of a curve, as shown in figure 4.11. When we represent a sound by a curve of this sort, we mean that it has a complex wave, with an infinite number of components. The height of the curve at any point represents the relative amplitude of the component with that frequency.

It is outside the scope of this book to give a complete mathematical explanation showing why there are an infinite number of components in the spectrum of a nonrepetitive wave. However, we may note in passing that the wave shown in figure 4.9, which had components of 900, 1,000, and 1,100 Hz, had a fundamental frequency of

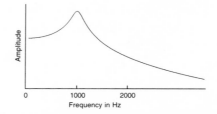

Fig. 4.11. The usual way of representing the spectrum of the nonrepetitive waveform shown in fig. 4.6.

100 Hz, i.e., it repeated itself every one-hundredth of a second. If the components had been 900, 950, 1,000, 1,050, and 1,100, i.e., spaced 50 Hz apart, the fundamental frequency would have been 50 Hz, since the waveform would have been repeated every one-fiftieth of a second. If we add still more components, so that they were, say, only 1 Hz apart, with frequencies of 900, 901, 902, 903, . . . 1,096, 1,097, 1,098, 1,099, and 1,100 Hz, we find that the complex wave produced has a fundamental frequency of 1 Hz. In order to produce a complex wave which repeats itself even more slowly, we must add component frequencies which are even closer together. If the waveform is to occur only once in an infinite amount of time, i.e., if it is never to repeat itself, then the components must be infinitely close together.

The spectra shown in figures 4.10 and 4.11 have peaks at 1,000 Hz, as might be expected for a waveform that has a tendency to repeat every one-thousandth of a second. Note also that the spectra are asymmetrical. The components below 1,000 Hz have a higher amplitude than components an equal distance above 1,000 Hz. These larger amplitudes are counterbalanced by the greater number of components above 1,000 Hz.

It was pointed out at the end of the preceding chapter

that most of the sounds with which we are concerned are neither nonrepetitive waveforms preceded and followed by silence, nor waves with a precise frequency of repetition. Instead they consist of waves which are more or less like the waves before and after them, the degree of their resemblance depending on the rate at which the quality is changing. Some speech sounds, such as vowels which continue for a comparatively long time, contain a number of consecutive waves which are almost identical to one another. Other parts of words, such as the abrupt beginning and end of the word *peak,* consist of sounds whose waveforms are altering very rapidly.

When we describe a sound wave by analyzing it into its components, we can either assume that it is one of an infinite number of identical waves (which is what we did in all our first analyses of complex waves), or we can assume that it is an isolated pressure variation, preceded and followed by silence (which, as we have just seen, leads us to the conclusion that it has an infinite number of components). When we are analyzing a sound wave which is one of a number of similar consecutive waves, we usually use the first method. The sound is then said to have a line spectrum; on the other hand, when each wave is quite different from the adjacent waves, it is normally analyzed by the second method. It is then said to have a continuous spectrum.

Earlier, we stated that it is convenient to regard all sounds as belonging to one or other of two classes, the one class having waveforms that recur at regular intervals of time and the other having nonrepetitive waveforms. We can now see how this distinction is made in practice. We usually consider a sound to have a repetitive waveform as opposed to a waveform which consists of random variations in air pressure if it is convenient to describe that particular sound by means of a line spectrum as opposed to a continuous spectrum. From a strictly mathematical point of view, all sounds should be described as having continuous spectra, as, in fact, all sounds have waveforms which are strictly speaking non-repetitive. But many sounds have waveforms which are so nearly exactly repetitive that we find it convenient to be able to describe them in terms of line spectra. When we analyze a nearly repetitive waveform in this way, we obtain a simplified description in which the more important components are accurately specified, and only very minor components are neglected.

Figure 4.12 shows the analysis of various waves in both forms. Three different waves are shown on the left of the diagram, and the spectrum corresponding to each of them is shown on the right. The vertical lines in the spectra represent the components which could be considered as being present if the corresponding wave was not just a single cycle but rather a cycle that was repeated an infinite number of times. The dotted curves in the diagrams of the spectra represent the results of the second form of analysis, in which the wave shown is considered to be a particular variation in air pressure that is preceded and followed by silence.

The wave illustrated at the top of figure 4.12 is nearly a pure tone. There is only a small decrease in amplitude between one peak and the next, and when the second cycle starts, the amplitude of the first peak in this cycle is not much greater than the last peak in the first cycle. Consequently, as we can see from the line spectrum, much of the energy of the complex wave is contained in the one component at 1,000 Hz. The additional components which have to be combined with it have very small amplitudes. Similar information is conveyed in another way by

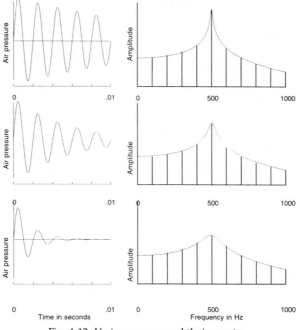

Fig. 4.12. Various waves and their spectra.

the continuous spectrum in which we can see from the sharpness of the curve that most of the energy is concentrated in one frequency region. The second wave in figure 4.12 has a slightly more rapid rate of decay. Its line spectrum shows that it is composed of a greater number of tones with an appreciable amplitude; or as we can see from the shape of the curve, the energy is not concentrated in such a narrow frequency region. The third wave dies away extremely rapidly. The amplitudes of the peaks in the first cycle are virtually zero just before the second cycle starts. Many components of almost equal amplitudes are needed in order to synthesize a complex wave-form of this sort; in other words, the energy is spread over a wide range of frequencies.

Now we can see one reason why we can consider a tuning fork to be almost a pure tone. The rate of decay of a tuning fork is very slow, slower even than that of the first wave in figure 4.12. It is possible to strike a tuning fork of, say, the note A (440 Hz), so that it lasts for several seconds. Consequently it makes many thousand vibrations, each being nearly the same as the preceding, and each having the smoothly increasing and decreasing curve shape that is associated with a sine wave. As a result, the waveform of a tuning fork can be analyzed into one dominant pure tone with negligible additional components.

Many of the sounds of speech, on the other hand, die away within a few thousandths of a second. They are similar to the third wave in figure 4.12, and on analysis prove to be composed of a large number of tones with similar amplitudes.

The general rule to be remembered is that a sharp pointed curve represents the spectrum of a sound with a slow rate of decay. As the energy in this sound is concentrated in one frequency region, it is nearly a pure tone. On the other hand, a nonrepetitive waveform with a rapid rate of decay is represented by a much flatter curve, indicating that it contains energy spread over a wider range of frequencies.

Many speech sounds consist of regular repetitions of a cycle of variations in air pressure that are fairly similar to the pressure variations considered in figure 4.12. At that time we noted that although only a single cycle was shown, it could be taken as representing a cycle that was repeated a number of times. Figure 4.13 shows on

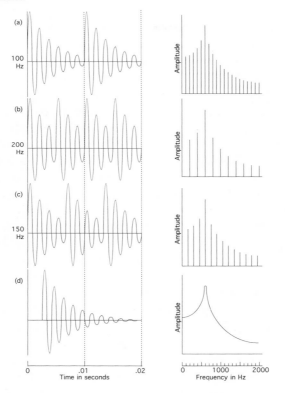

Fig. 4.13. Various waves and their spectra.

the left three further waves of this type, plus a fourth wave which may be considered as being preceded and followed by silence. If this fourth wave represents the sound produced by a single tap on a body of air, then the other waves represent sounds produced by a series of taps recurring at regular intervals of time. As we shall see later, these "taps" correspond in speech sounds to the regular opening and closing of the vocal folds.

The wave at the top left of figure 4.13 has a fundamental frequency of 100 Hz. As you can see from the time scale at the bottom of the figure, one cycle occurs in .01 seconds. Within each cycle there are six peaks, corresponding to a wave with six times the fundamental frequency. We may therefore expect the 600 Hz component to have a relatively high amplitude. Earlier in this chapter we saw that when we analyze a repetitive wave so as to produce a line spectrum, we find that all the components have frequencies that are whole-number multiples of the frequency of repetition of the complex waveform. So, in the case of the first wave in figure 4.13, the possible components are tones with frequencies of 100, 200, 300, . . . Hz. The actual spectrum of this wave is shown on the right of the figure. The largest component is, as expected, the one at 600 Hz.

Similar peaks recur every 1/600 second in the wave at the bottom of figure 4.13. But, as this wave is considered to be preceded and followed by silence, it is analyzed in terms of a continuous spectrum. In this spectrum, just as in the spectrum of the first wave, the component with the largest amplitude has a frequency of 600 Hz. There are, moreover, other similarities between the spectra of these two waves: the relative amplitudes of all the components in the spectrum of the first wave are exactly the same as the relative amplitudes of the corresponding components in the last wave.

When we consider the second and third waves in figure 4.13, we find that their spectra are also in some ways similar to the spectrum of the last wave. The second wave (b) is a complex waveform recurring twice in one-hundredth of a second. Consequently it has a fundamental frequency of 200 Hz, and the harmonics in its spectra are multiples of 200. The third harmonic forms the peak in the spectrum.

The third wave recurs three times in .02 seconds, which gives it a fundamental frequency of 150 Hz. In this case it is the fourth harmonic that forms the peak at 600 Hz in the spectrum. As in the case of the other waves, all the components that are present have the same relative amplitudes in the spectrum. We could draw an identical curve round the spectrum of each of the first three waves; moreover, this curve has the same shape as the spectrum of the last wave, which is an isolated occurrence of a waveform similar to the repetitive waveforms contained in each of the other waves. This result will be important for us when we come to consider how the phonetic quality of a sound may stay the same despite variations in the pitch, which is, of course, dependent on the fundamental frequency.

We may conclude this chapter by considering the components that we would have to combine in order to build up the irregular waveforms that occur during the sounds at the ends of the words *hiss* and *hush*. If you listen to these two sounds you will hear that they both convey some sensation of pitch. They both have energy spread

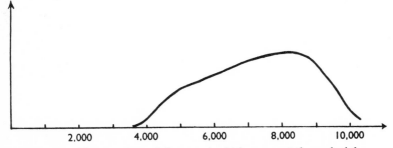

Fig. 4.14. The spectrum of the sound which occurs at the end of the word *hiss*. In this and all following figures showing spectra the horizontal scale gives the frequency in Hz; the vertical dimension indicates the relative amplitude of the components.

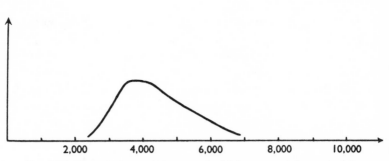

Fig. 4.15. The spectrum of the sound which occurs at the end of the word *hush*.

over a wide range of frequencies; but in neither case is it completely uniformly divided among the frequency components. Their spectra are shown in figures 4.14 and 4.15. In the sound at the end of the word *hiss*, most of the component frequencies with any appreciable amplitude are above 6,600 Hz. The sound at the end of *hush*, on the other hand, has a substantial amount of its energy divided among frequency components from about 3,000 Hz to about 4,500 Hz. It is accordingly heard as the lower pitched of these two sounds.

CHAPTER FIVE
Resonance

In the last few chapters the emphasis has been on the analysis of sound waves rather than on their production. We must now consider some of the properties of sources of sounds.

All sources of sound are moving bodies. Some of them, like tuning forks and piano strings, have a natural tendency to vibrate. Once they have been struck they go on vibrating at a definite rate (or frequency) for a considerable time. Other sources of sound, like drums and table tops, have less tendency to vibrate. They make a noise when struck, but the vibrations die away fairly rapidly. Still other sources, such as telephone earpieces and loudspeakers, have virtually no natural frequency of vibration. Each move backward and forward has to be controlled by electric currents.

It is, of course, possible to make one vibrating body cause vibrations in another body. This happens when the base of a sounding fork is placed on the table. If you strike a tuning fork and then hold it in your hand while it is vibrating, it makes only a soft sound. But as soon as you place the base of the fork on a table, the sound becomes very much louder. The movements of the fork cannot cause large variations in air pressure because the prongs are fairly small, and the air, instead of being compressed, can easily move around the sides of the prongs. But when the base of the fork is placed on a table, the vibrations of the fork are transmitted to the table, which then vibrates so that a larger amount of air is affected. The energy which the fork is expending in its vibrations is changed into sound waves more efficiently by the large flat space of the table.

This principle is employed in many musical instruments. A vibrating string does not by itself cause a very large disturbance of the air. But when, as in a piano or a violin, the vibrations of the string are made to drive a sounding board or the body of the violin, a much louder sound results. However, we must note that neither the sounding board nor the body of the violin vibrates in the same way as the strings which are driving it. To some extent each prefers its own natural mode of vibration.

We are all familiar with several objects other than musical instruments which have a tendency to vibrate at specific frequencies. Glasses, vases, and many other objects will give out a ringing note when struck. These objects will also resound when the appropriate note is played on a piano. A glass can even be made to ring if a person sings a suitable note. It is often said that opera singers, who can sing an appropriate note very loudly and clearly, can make a glass vibrate so much that it shatters of its own accord. I must admit that I have never witnessed this event happening.

A simpler example of this sort of phenomenon can be demonstrated with two identical tuning forks. If one fork is struck and then brought near another fork whose natural frequency of vibration is the same, the second fork will begin to vibrate. As soon as the second fork has been set in motion, it will, of course, create a sound wave in the ordinary way. Even if you stop the first fork by placing a finger upon it, the second fork, once it has been started, will go on vibrating until it comes to rest of its own accord. This phenomenon, whereby one body can be set in motion by the vibrations of another body, is known as resonance. The one body is said to resonate to the other body.

It is easy enough to understand how resonance occurs in the case of the two tuning forks. When the first fork has been struck, it vibrates, causing variations in air pressure to spread outward. These pressure variations are, as we have seen, the result of small movements of particles of air. When the pressure variations occur alongside the second fork, the air particles there are vibrating in much the same way as the original fork. These movements act as a series of small pushes on the second fork, which is consequently set in motion.

It is important to note that the second fork does not start sounding loudly as soon as the first fork has been struck. It takes a certain amount of time for the vibrations to build up to their maximum. The air particles move in such a way that each back-and-forth movement acts as a small blow whose effect is added to that of the previous blow. Because the two tuning forks have the same natural frequency of vibration, each of these small blows arrives at exactly the right moment, so that its effect is to increase the total amount of vibration.

We can perhaps make this clearer by considering a parallel case which is more familiar. Suppose you wished to give a child a ride on a swing. You would begin by giving a small push so that the swing would move away from you. Then, when it had swung back toward you again and was at the top of its curve, you would give it another small push. This would increase the amplitude of its swing; and on the next occasion another small push would make the child swing even higher. With a number of small pushes you can build up a large movement of the swing. But it all depends on the timing of the small pushes or blows. If you tried to give the small added push to the swing when it was still coming toward you, you would slow it down and not assist it. Only if you wait until the swing is about to move away from you can your push have the maximum effect. This is the situation with the two identical tuning forks. The first small blow imparts a very slight motion to the second tuning fork. But this fork, having been displaced from its position of rest, moves back again with its natural rate of vibration and is just about to start a second swing when the second blow occurs. This blow and all the subsequent ones help to build up large vibrations. But obviously the second fork will vibrate only if the blows arrive at the appropriate moments. This will occur if the natural rates of vibration (or frequencies) of the tuning forks are the same.

We may now consider more complex cases of resonance, such as that of a glass ringing when the appropriate note is struck on a piano. Basically the same principle is in operation. The piano causes movements of the air particles, which set the glass vibrating. As we saw in the last chapter, the sound wave produced by a piano has a complex form. The spectrum (fig. 4.4) shows that it is composed of a fundamental and a large number of harmonics, some of which are fairly powerful. If one of these components has the same frequency as the natural rate of vibration of the glass, it can cause movements of the air which set the glass vibrating.

It may, at first, seem hard to understand that the sound waves produced by a piano are actually, in practice, equivalent to a number of simple waves. But this is in fact the case. A numerical example may make the matter clearer. Let us suppose we have a glass whose natural frequency of vibration is 1,046 Hz. When a note with this frequency (c″) is played on a piano, the glass will be set vibrating. But it will also vibrate when the note c′ (523 Hz) is played. A piano note of this frequency contains a strong second harmonic, i.e., a component with a frequency of 2 × 523 Hz. Because of this there will be appropriately timed movements of the air particles which can start the glass vibrating. The movements of the air particles corresponding to the fundamental frequency of 523 Hz will alternately reinforce and oppose these movements, and will do just as much of one as of the other. Nor will the higher harmonics have any appreciable adverse effect. Consequently the glass will be set vibrating with its own frequency, which is that of the second harmonic.

In previous chapters we saw that a sound consists essentially of variations in air pressure due to small movements of the particles of air, which are in their turn caused by movements of the source of sound. Consequently a diagram of a sound wave, such as that in figure 5.1, can be regarded as representing either variations in air pressure or movements of the source of sound. Similarly the corresponding spectrum gives an indication of the components we would have to use to build up the complex wave; and it also provides a description of the natural frequencies of vibration of the source of sound. These are, of course, the frequencies to which the source of sound will respond when it is acting as a resonator. So we can see that figure 5.1 can be regarded in two ways: it shows not only the composition of the complex wave produced by the sound source but also the frequencies at which the sound source resonates most easily. In this

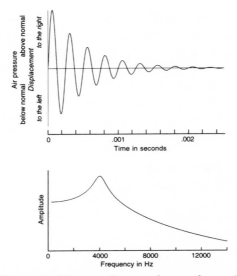

Fig. 5.1. Upper part of figure: a diagram of a sound wave (and of the movements of the source of sound producing the sound wave). Lower part of figure: the spectrum of this sound wave (and of the movements of the source of sound).

case it would respond best to frequencies around 4,000 Hz (which is the basic component in the complex wave); it would be slightly affected by frequencies around 3,000 and 4,500 Hz (regions in which there are somewhat smaller components in the complex wave); but it would hardly respond at all to frequencies above 3,000 Hz, a region in which there is scarcely any energy in the complex wave. This principle applies to all sources of sounds. The spectra of the sounds they emit when undergoing free vibrations is also an indication of the frequencies to which they will respond.

As a further example of this phenomenon we may consider a tuning fork, whose spectrum is a sharply peaked curve. As we saw in the last chapter, this indicates that all the energy is concentrated in one narrow frequency region, i.e., it is very nearly a pure tone. Consequently a tuning fork will resonate only to a sound wave containing this frequency. As we also saw, it is characteristic of a sharply peaked spectrum that it should indicate a source of sound which takes a long time to decay. Equally well, when the tuning fork is acting as a resonator—perhaps resonating to another tuning fork in the way we have already discussed—it takes a comparatively long time for its vibrations to build up.

If we make the vibrations of a tuning fork die away more quickly, perhaps by lightly touching it with a piece of cotton wool, we alter the quality of the sound wave that it produces. In addition we alter the way in which it will respond when it is acting as a resonator. We saw at the end of chapter 4 that sounds with a more rapid rate of decay have their energy dispersed among a greater range of frequencies. A tuning fork whose vibrations are being made to decay more rapidly will produce a complex wave with a number of component frequencies. Equally well, it will resonate when it is in the presence of any of these frequencies.

A source of sound whose vibrations die away quickly is said to be damped. A nonrepetitive waveform which decays very rapidly is called a highly damped sound. The sounding board of a piano and the body of a violin are examples of damped resonators. Tuning forks are, for practical purposes, undamped sources of sound (although, theoretically, the slight air resistance and other frictional forces which eventually do slow them down might be classified as damping forces).

We can now restate our conclusions about resonators in a different form: damped resonators, whose vibrations build up and die away quickly, can be set in motion by a wide range of frequencies, i.e., they are described by flat curves. Undamped resonators, on the other hand, require a longer time for their vibrations to build up and to die away; they can be set in motion by a limited range of frequencies only, i.e., they are described by sharply peaked curves.

The curve describing the way in which a resonator will vibrate in response to any given frequency is called the resonance curve. So that we can see the sort of information conveyed by these curves, we may consider the case of a slightly damped resonator, whose curve is shown in the center of figure 5.2. (This curve, of course, is also a description of the complex wave which would be produced by the resonator.) Now let us suppose that we try to make it respond by producing three pure tones. Let us assume that the frequencies of these three tones are 250 Hz, 300 Hz, and 375 Hz, but that all have the same amplitude (i.e., all have peaks of excess pressure of the same size). The resonator will be set in vibration by each of these tones. But it prefers to vibrate at a frequency of 300 Hz. Consequently the 300 Hz tone will cause the largest vibrations; the size (or amplitude) of the vibrations which the resonator will make in response to this tone can be represented by the line *b*. Although the 250 Hz tone has the same amplitude as the 300 Hz tone, it will not cause such large vibrations, as this is not the preferred frequency of the resonator. When the resonator is set in motion by the 250 Hz tone, it will vibrate with an amplitude represented by the line *a*, i.e., in proportion to the size of the 250 Hz tone in its complex wave. Similarly, we can deduce from the curve the size of the vibrations which the resonator will make when it is set in motion by the 375 Hz tone. The resonator has hardly any natural tendency to

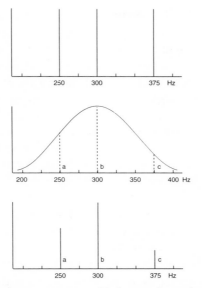

Fig. 5.2. When three pure tones with frequencies and amplitudes as shown in the upper part of the figure are applied separately to a system which has a resonance curve as shown in the middle part of the figure, then the system will vibrate with the frequencies and amplitudes shown in the lower part of the figure.

vibrate at this frequency—the 375 Hz component in its complex wave has a very small amplitude. Consequently a 375 Hz tone will cause only small vibrations of the resonator, their amplitude being represented by the short line c. The size of the resonator's vibrations at any frequency will depend on the extent to which this frequency is present in its complex wave. This is what is meant by saying that the resonance curve of a body has the same shape as its spectrum.

The resonator whose curve is shown in figure 5.2 can be set in vibration effectively by tones with frequencies from about 250 Hz to about 350 Hz. Compared with this, the resonance curve shown in figure 5.1 represents a resonator that will respond effectively to a much wider range of frequencies—from somewhere around 3,000 Hz to about 5,000 Hz. It is often necessary in acoustics to specify the range that can cause a resonator to vibrate. You can, if you like, regard this as a kind of measure of the sensitivity of a resonator. A tuning fork is sensitive to a very narrow range of frequencies, whereas a damped resonator can be set in motion by a much wider range. But it is difficult to give a precise specification of the band of frequencies that can be used to set a resonator in vibration, because of the way in which resonance curves taper away. The resonator discussed in the previous paragraph, for instance, can be set in motion by frequencies of 375 Hz and over; but its vibrations in response to frequencies in this range will be very small, and can be discounted for most practical purposes.

The sounds which we use to try to set a resonator in motion are known as the input to the resonator. The way in which the resonator vibrates in response to these sounds is known as its output for a given input. Now suppose that the input to a resonator consists of a very large number of tones, all with equal amplitudes. Such an input can be represented by the spectrum in figure 5.3. If the resonator in question has a curve with a peak of 800 Hz, as shown in figure 5.4., its output will be a sound with the spectrum shown in figure 5.5. It will resonate with maximum efficiency to the 800 Hz tone (which is known as the resonant frequency), and with decreasing efficiency to tones on either side of that frequency.

One conventional way of stating the frequency range within which a resonator will respond effectively is to consider the frequencies at which the amplitude of the

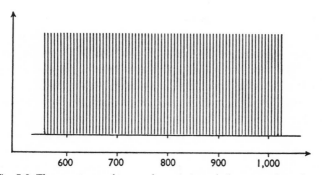

Fig. 5.3. The spectrum of a sound consisting of a large number of tones with the same amplitude.

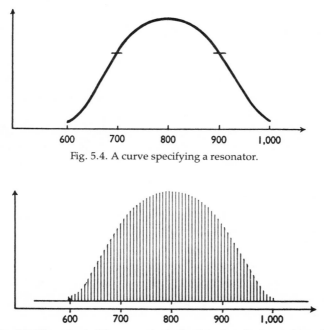

Fig. 5.4. A curve specifying a resonator.

Fig. 5.5. The output of the resonator in fig. 5.4 when the input shown in fig. 5.3 is applied to it.

output is 70.7% of the output at the resonant frequency. The reason why this particular value is chosen will become apparent shortly. For the resonator in question, the outputs at 700 Hz and at 900 Hz will be 70.7% of the output at 800 Hz, although the inputs at these three frequencies were all the same. Accordingly we may consider this resonator to be effective within this range. Any frequency between 700 Hz and 900 Hz will set up vibrations whose amplitude will be at least 0.707 of the amplitude of the vibrations caused by an 800 Hz. tone of equal strength.

The effective frequency range of a resonator is known as its bandwidth. Diagrams of resonators with bandwidths of 10 Hz (from 95 to 105 Hz), 50 Hz (from 175 to 225 Hz), and 200 Hz (from 350 to 550 Hz) are shown in figure 5.6. As you can see, the peaks of the resonance curves are at 100 Hz, 200 Hz, and 450 Hz; frequencies up to 5 Hz, 25 Hz, and 100 Hz on either side of these peaks will produce outputs with at least 70.7% of the amplitude of the output at the resonant frequency.

When we analyze sounds we use resonators (or computers which simulate resonators) to tell us which frequencies are present. There is a difficulty in designing resonators for this purpose. As we have stressed, resonators with a narrow bandwidth (i.e., with sharply peaked resonance curves) respond to a small range of frequencies, but they take a comparatively long time for the amplitude of their vibrations to build up, and they also have a slower rate of decay. They may tell us precisely what frequencies are present in a sound wave, but they take a certain amount of time to do it. Conversely, resonators that will respond to a broad range of frequencies build up to their maximum amplitude far more quickly. They may not tell us the precise frequency of a component of a com-

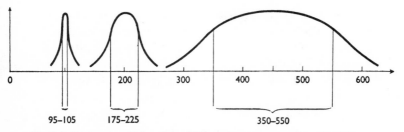

Fig. 5.6. Curves specifying three different resonators, each with a different center frequency and a different bandwidth.

plex wave, but they need less time to produce the information.

It is because of this that there is a problem in designing a resonator that will respond to a given frequency. Let us suppose, for example, that we wanted to know whether there was a component with a frequency of 500 Hz in a certain speech sound. A resonator that was sensitive to a narrow band of frequencies around 500 Hz would require a certain amount of time to respond. But the speech sound in question might not last that long. Consequently we should have to use a resonator that responds more quickly, which of course means that it also responds to a wider range of frequencies. We can tell the precise frequencies that are present in a sound only if we have sufficient time for a resonator with a small bandwidth to be set in vibration.

The same principle applies irrespective of whether we are using actual resonators or computers to analyze a sound. The computer must take in a certain length of sound. The longer the length that is analyzed, the more accurately can the component frequencies be determined. As we will discuss in a later section, in a typical computer analysis we might look at about 50 milliseconds of a sound and be able to determine component frequencies to the nearest 40 Hz. Alternatively, we might consider a longer period, say about 100 milliseconds of the same sound; then we would be able to determine component frequencies to the nearest 20 Hz. We would, of course, be finding the average frequency components over the whole 100 millisecond period, which is about half the length of a typical syllable. If we wanted to know how the frequencies differed in the first quarter of a syllable, we would have to be satisfied with an analysis that determined the component frequencies only to the nearest 40 Hz. It is a fact of life that one can either know fairly precisely when a sound occurred, or one can tell fairly precisely what frequencies were present.

Most of the resonators with which we have been concerned have been vibrating bodies, such as tuning forks and piano strings. But it is also possible for a body of air to vibrate and hence to act as a source of sound or a resonator. This is what happens when you make a bottle sound by blowing across the top of it. The human voice, the organ, and many other instruments make use of a vibrating air column.

When we were considering the transmission of sound in chapter 1, we saw that air could become compressed and rarefied. If it is suitably contained it can, in fact, behave in a similar way to a coiled spring. You can make a spring vibrate by giving it a light tap; the rate of the vibrations will be dependent mainly on the size and stiffness of the spring. Similarly, the air in a tube can be set vibrating if it is suitably excited. The rate at which a body of air will vibrate depends upon its size and its elasticity (the factor corresponding to the stiffness of the coiled spring). Normally the elasticity can be regarded as a fixed physical constant; but the size of a body of air can, of course, be altered. As in the case of the coiled spring, a large body of air vibrates more slowly than a small body of air contained in a similar way.

Figure 5.7 shows a typical laboratory arrangement for producing a vibrating column of air. The effective length of the tube can be adjusted by increasing or decreasing the amount of water it contains. When the length is such that the natural rate of vibration of the body of air is the same as that of a tuning fork which is held above it, resonance will occur. Just as in the other examples of resonance, small movements of the tuning fork will act as a series of blows which will eventually build up large movements of the body of air. This movement will cause

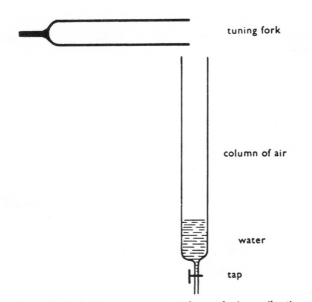

tuning fork

column of air

water

tap

Fig. 5.7. A typical laboratory arrangement for producing a vibrating column of air.

a disturbance in the surrounding air, which will, of course, spread outward in the form of sound waves.

The air in a container usually vibrates in a complex manner. Among the factors which influence the form of the complex wave is the shape of the container. For example, a bottle with a thin neck and a large body has a lower fundamental frequency than a wide-necked bottle somewhat smaller in size. Resonating air columns are of great importance from our point of view, because the differences between many speech sounds are due to the varying shape of the body of air contained in the mouth and throat. We will consider the vibrations of the air in the vocal tract in chapters 7 and 8.

If we sound a whole series of tuning forks above an empty pipe, some will have no effect at all, whereas others will set the air inside it vibrating. Now let us suppose that this pipe went through a wall. Then when some tuning forks were sounded alongside the pipe, listeners in the other room would hear nothing, other tuning forks they would hear slightly, and yet others would sound quite loud. A fork would sound loud to the hearer depending on the extent to which the air in the pipe was set in motion by that fork.

When a resonator is behaving in this way we call it an acoustic filter. A filter is a resonator which is used to transmit or pass on sound, and which is selective with respect to frequency; in other words, it transmits one frequency with greater efficiency than another. The range of frequencies that a filter will pass on is known as the bandwidth of the filter. If the input to a filter consists of a large number of different frequencies, all with the same amplitude, then its bandwidth is said to be the range of frequencies that it will pass on with at least 70.7% of the amplitude of the frequency which it passes with maxi-

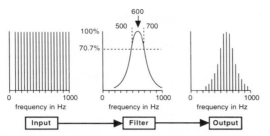

Fig. 5.8. The input and output for a filter with a center frequency of 600 Hz and a bandwidth of 200 Hz.

mum efficiency. (The reason for the choice of the value 70.7% will be explained in the next chapter.)

Schematically we can consider a filter to be a device such as that shown in the middle of figure 5.8. This is a system into which we might put a range of frequencies such as that represented by the spectrum on the left of the figure, a set of tones all of the same amplitude and with frequencies 50 Hz apart from 100 Hz to 1,000 Hz. The filter will then pass those frequencies that are present in its resonance curve, so that its output will be as shown in the spectrum on the right of the figure. In this case the filter has a center frequency of 600 Hz and a bandwidth of 200 Hz. In other words, it will output frequencies between 500 and 700 Hz so that they have at least 70.7% of the amplitude of a tone with a frequency of 600 Hz and the same input amplitude. The resonant frequencies of a filter can be said to constitute a pole, so that the simple filter we have been considering can be said to have a pole with a frequency of 600 Hz and a bandwidth of 200 Hz.

CHAPTER SIX

Hearing

All students of speech need to be acquainted with some of the facts of hearing. We may begin by considering the perceived pitch of different sounds. In the previous chapters we have presumed that the pitch sensation of a sound is directly dependent on the frequency of the wave. This assumption needs some qualification, as a variation in the amplitude of the wave will also affect the pitch sensation. The nature of this effect depends on the frequency of the sound in question. As a rough rule we can say that as the amplitude of any sound with a fundamental frequency above 1,500 Hz increases, the sound will become not only louder but also higher in pitch. Conversely, if we increase the amplitude of a sound below 1,500 Hz, the pitch of the sound will be heard as lower. You can try this effect for yourself by sounding a tuning fork of, say, 200 Hz and moving it backward and forward near your ear. When it is close to your ear, it will sound not only louder but also slightly lower in pitch than when it is further away. Another way of doing this experiment is to vary the volume control on a radio set while listening to a tuning signal. If the frequency of the tuning signal is below 1,500 Hz, then when you turn the volume control up, the pitch of the sound will be heard as lower. However, as you will see if you try these experiments, variations in amplitude do not have a very great effect on the pitch of a sound, so that for most practical purposes we can still say that the pitch that we hear depends on the frequency of the wave form.

The perceived pitch of a complex sound depends, not on the frequency of the component with the largest amplitude, but on the fundamental frequency of repetition of the complex wave. For example, consider a wave with three components as shown in the upper part of figure 6.1, one of them being a 100 Hz wave with a very small amplitude and the other two being waves with frequencies of 200 Hz and 300 Hz and larger amplitudes. The complex wave has a fundamental frequency of 100 Hz. Consequently the pitch of this waveform will be the same as that of a pure tone with a frequency of 100 Hz and a comparable amplitude. The fact that the second and third harmonics both have a greater amplitude than that of the fundamental frequency is of no consequence as far as the perceived pitch of the sound is concerned.

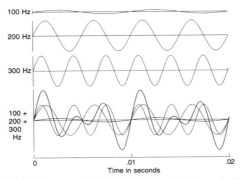

Fig. 6.1. The combination of a 100 Hz wave with a very small amplitude and waves of 200 Hz and 300 Hz with larger amplitudes.

It is even possible that when we make a frequency analysis of a complex wave, we may find that there is no component with a frequency which is the same as the frequency of repetition of the complex wave. If the waveform shown in figure 6.2 continued indefinitely, it could be analyzed into components with frequencies of 1,800, 2,000, and 2,200 Hz. But the complex waveform repeats itself 200 times a second (i.e., from *a* to *b* is 1/200 of a second). Consequently, the perceived pitch of this sound will be the same as that of a pure tone with a frequency of 200 Hz, although the complex wave can be said to have only an imaginary component with this frequency. (Another way of looking at the frequency analysis of this complex wave is to say that there are components with frequencies of 200, 400, 600, 800, . . . , and all the other whole-number multiples of 200, but only three of these components—those with frequencies of 1,800, 2,000, and 2,200 Hz—have any amplitude.)

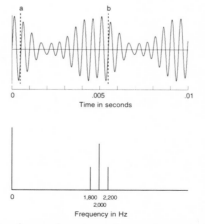

Fig. 6.2. The waveform and spectrum of a complex wave with a pitch the same as that of a pure tone of 200 Hz.

Because the ear detects pitch in this way, we can often remove all the lower-frequency components in a complex wave without affecting the perceived pitch. We could, for example, pass a complex wave with a fundamental frequency of 100 Hz through a filter which cuts out all the frequencies below 500 Hz. As long as some of the higher-frequency components are still separated from one another by 100 Hz, the complex wave will still be repeated 100 times a second, and the pitch that we hear will be unaltered. In fact, an ordinary telephone circuit does not pass much energy below 300 Hz. This will affect the quality of the sound (as the quality depends on the way in which the energy is distributed among the frequency components), but the perceived pitch will remain the same, even if it is well below 300 Hz.

In this book we are not concerned with the physiology of hearing. The function of the ear is to turn sound waves, which are an acoustic form of energy, into nerve impulses, which are an electrochemical form of energy that can be handled within the brain. The way in which this happens is outside our scope. But it is interesting to note that physiologists have shown that the ear produces a pattern of impulses which corresponds to some kind of frequency analysis of the complex wave, and an additional series of impulses corresponding in part to the rate of repetition of the complex wave. In all probability, what we hear as the quality of a sound is largely dependent on the first set of impulses, whereas the perceived pitch of speech sounds depends on the second.

The ear is capable of distinguishing between a large number of different pitches. How many pitch differences can be determined depends on the experimental technique used. In one type of laboratory experiment, it has been shown that the variation in frequency which we can just detect as a change in pitch is about 2 or 3 Hz in notes with frequencies below 1,000 Hz. For higher notes, an increasingly large change has to be made before we hear any variation in pitch. A set of values for the sensitivity of the ear to changes in frequency is shown in figure 6.3. As you can see, the change in frequency in higher notes that can just be heard as a change in pitch is a more or less constant proportion—about 1/500, or 0.2% of the frequency of the sound. Thus the just noticeable difference in frequency at 3,000 Hz is about $0.002 \times 3,000$, i.e., 6 Hz; and at 7,000 it is nearly $0.002 \times 7,000$, i.e., 14 Hz. We are not quite so good at detecting changes in complex sounds such as vowels. There has to be a change of about 8 Hz in a component at 1,000 Hz before we can hear a change in quality.

As the ear is more sensitive to changes in frequency in the lower part of the scale, the difference in pitch between notes with frequencies of 600 and 700 Hz will be greater than the difference between notes of 3,600 and 3,700 Hz. Between the first pair of notes there will be

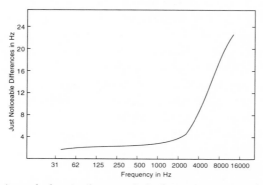

Fig. 6.3. A graph showing how much the frequency or a tone has to be altered in order to produce a change in pitch.

about thirty-five just noticeable differences in frequency, but between the higher pair there will be only fourteen. In this region notes must be separated by approximately 250 Hz to make a difference in pitch comparable to the difference between 600 and 700 Hz.

You can observe this effect for yourself by playing notes on a piano. Play a pair of notes separated by two other notes at the bass end of a piano; now play a pair of notes similarly separated by two notes at the treble end. The first pair of notes will sound distinctly farther apart than the second pair.

We often want to represent a difference in perceived pitch between notes by means of points on a diagram or graph which shows differences in frequency. For many purposes it would be convenient if we could represent equal intervals in pitch by equally spaced points on the graph. To do this we want to know the relation between the frequency of a note and its height on the pitch scale. This relationship has been found by various psychological experiments, all of which show that the ear actually behaves in a very complex way. But as a rough rule we can say that the perceived pitch of a note increases linearly with its frequency between 100 and 1,000 Hz, so that, for example, the difference in pitch between notes with frequencies of 300 and 450 Hz is much the same as the differences between notes with frequencies of 450 and 600 Hz, and 750 and 900 Hz. But between 1,000 and 10,000 Hz, the relation between the pitch we hear and the actual frequency of a note is what mathematicians call *logarithmic*; this means that the pitch interval between two notes in this range depends on the ratio of the two frequencies, so that, for example, from 1,500 to 3,000 Hz (a ratio of 1 to 2) and from 4,000 to 8,000 (also a ratio of 1 to 2) are equal intervals of pitch (although the first pair of notes are separated by 1,500 Hz, as compared to the 4,000 Hz that separate the second pair).

A more accurate way of representing differences in pitch is by means of the mel or bark scales. The mel is defined as the unit of pitch such that when pairs of sounds are separated by an equal number of mels, they are also separated by equal intervals of pitch. The unit is derived from numerous psychophysical experiments in which subjects were asked to perform tasks such as deciding when one tone was half the pitch of another, and when one tone was midway in pitch between two others. These experiments enabled a graph to be drawn showing the relation between the frequency of a note and its value on the mel scale. Another set of psychophysical experiments was used in producing the bark scale, which also reflects the ear's sensitivity to differences in pitch. In this case the basic technique was to determine the width of a band of noise within which a pure tone of a given frequency was no longer audible.

The mel scale and the bark scale present slightly different views of the relation between pitch and frequency. Table 6.1 shows the mel and the bark values of particular frequencies. Figure 6.4 shows the same data in graphical form. You can use this graph to find the mel or bark values of any frequency given in Hz. Thus it is apparent that 1,000 Hz is equal to 1,000 mels and about 8.5 bark; and 2,000 Hz is about 1,550 mels and 13 bark. Frequency data about speech sounds are often converted into mel or bark units before being presented graphically, the choice of which unit to choose being a matter of argument.

We may now turn to an examination of the loudness of different sounds. We have already seen that the loudness of a sound is dependent mainly on the amplitude of the wave. So far we have been using the term amplitude in a

Table 6.1 The Relation between Frequencies in hertz, mels, and bark

Frequency in Hz	Pitch in Mels	Frequency in Hz	Pitch in Bark
20	0	20	0
160	250	100	1
394	500	200	2
670	750	300	3
1,000	1,000	400	4
1,420	1,250	510	5
1,900	1,500	630	6
2,450	1,750	770	7
3,120	2,000	920	8
4,000	2,250	1,080	9
		1,270	10
		1,480	11
		1,720	12
		2,000	13
		2,320	14
		2,700	15
		3,150	16
		3,700	17
		4,400	18

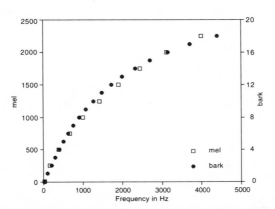

Fig. 6.4. Graph showing the relation between frequencies in Hz and the corresponding values on two different pitch scales, mel and bark.

general way to indicate any variation above or below normal air pressure. But let us suppose that we wish to compare the amplitudes of the two sounds whose waveforms are shown in figure 6.5. To make a valid comparison, we must consider not the maximum amplitudes but some sort of average of all the variations from normal pressure in each of these two waveforms. Now if we make a straightforward arithmetical average, the result may be zero, as every increase may be exactly matched by a subsequent decrease in pressure. Consequently it is useful to make use of a mathematical device which gives us another form of average, known as the rms. (root-mean-square) value, which is more in keeping with our commonsense ideas about the average amplitudes of these two waveforms. If you are not particularly good at mathematics you can simply regard the rms. amplitude as a useful form of average of the variations in pressure in a sound and not worry about the details of the method. The way in which we arrive at this average is to square

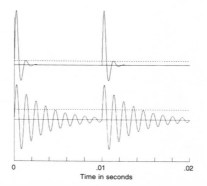

Fig. 6.5. Two complex waves. When comparing the loudness of these two sounds we must consider the rms amplitudes (shown by dashed lines) rather than the peak amplitudes.

the values of all the points through which the line passes (which turns them all into positive values, as, e.g., -2 times -2 equals $+4$), then take the mean (or average) of these values, and then take the square root of this quantity. This value is a measure of the average variation in air pressure. The rms. values of the amplitudes of the waves shown in figure 6.5 are indicated by means of a dashed line. In the case of these two waves, the one which has the smaller peak amplitude (i.e., the smaller maximum variation in air pressure) has the larger rms. amplitude. As the loudness of a sound depends on the rms. amplitude and not on the peak amplitude, the first sound is louder than the second.

As long as we are concerned simply with stating whether one sound is louder than another, we need to know only whether the amplitude of the one is greater than the amplitude of the other. But if we want to say how much louder the one sound is, we must compare the power of the two sounds. The power of a sound depends on the square of the amplitude. Thus, if the amplitude of a sound is doubled, the power is increased by a factor of two squared, i.e., by four; and if the amplitude is then trebled, the power is increased ninefold, so that it is thirty-six times its original value. As we shall see, the differences in power between sounds are often enormous.

The actual value of the power of a sound can be specified precisely in the units used by physicists. Similarly, the amplitude can be sated in terms of the units which physicists use in their measurements of air pressure. A common practice is to define as a reference level a sound which has an amplitude of 0.0002 dynes per square centimeter, and a power of 10^{-16} watts per square centimeter. However, we need not worry about the nature of these units, as we are usually concerned not with the absolute values of the power or the amplitude of a sound but only their value in relation to other sounds. Once we have defined an arbitrary reference level we can consider the amplitude or the power of any sound as being so much larger or so much smaller than that of the reference sound.

The reference sound specified above is one which is not quite as loud as the quietest sound that can just be heard under suitable experimental conditions. The loudest sound that we can stand without a feeling of pain in our ears has more than 1,000,000,000,000 times more power than this (which means, of course, that its amplitude is over 1,000,000 times greater than that of the reference sound).

Figure 6.6 shows the powers of sounds constituting thirteen approximately equal steps of loudness, starting from the reference level and going up to the loudest note we can stand without a feeling of pain. As you can see, the difference in power (in actual watts per square centimeter) is far greater between steps twelve and thirteen than it is between steps one and two, or two and three; but the power ratio between any two adjacent steps remains the same.

It is partly because the differences in power among sounds are so large, and partly because the differences in loudness depend on the ratio of the powers rather than on the actual values, that acousticians have adopted the decibel scale. The difference in decibels between two sounds is defined as ten times the common logarithm of their power ratios. This is not really as complicated as it appears and should prove to be understandable even by those who have forgotten what is meant by a common logarithm. Table 6.2 will help to make the matter clearer.

As you can see, all you have to do to find the common

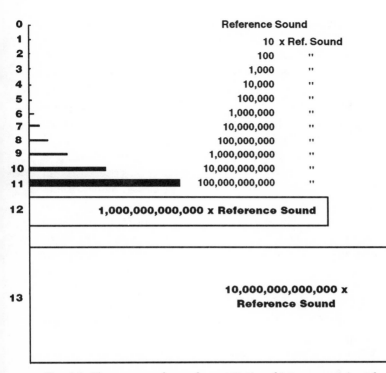

0		**Reference Sound**	
1		10	**x Ref. Sound**
2		100	"
3		1,000	"
4		10,000	"
5		100,000	"
6		1,000,000	"
7		10,000,000	"
8		100,000,000	"
9		1,000,000,000	"
10		10,000,000,000	"
11		100,000,000,000	"
12		**1,000,000,000,000 x Reference Sound**	
13		**10,000,000,000,000 x Reference Sound**	

Fig. 6.6. The powers of sounds constituting thirteen approximately equal steps of loudness. The power of each sound in watts per sq cm is proportional to the area of each block.

Table 6.2 The Relation between the Amplitude (Power) of a Sound and Its Relative Level in Decibels

Power Ratio between Sounds	Common Logarithm of the Power Ratio	Difference in Decibels
10 to 1	1	10
100 to 1	2	20
1,000 to 1	3	30

logarithm of the power ratios shown in the table is to count the number of zeroes. The difference in decibels between the two sounds can then be found by multiplying this number by ten. If we apply this method to the power ratios shown in figure 6.6, we find that the common logarithm of the power ratio between the greatest sound that the human ear can stand and the reference level is thirteen, since this number has thirteen zeroes in it. The difference in decibels (or dB to use the common abbreviation) between these two sounds is therefore ten times this, i.e., 130 dB. Similarly the difference in dB between, for example, steps three and five is 20 dB, since the power at step five is 100 times greater than it is at step three, and the common logarithm of 100 is two. This is, of course, the same as the difference between steps six and eight, or any other pair of steps which have a power ratio of 100 to 1.

By now you can probably see the advantages of using the decibel scale. Each step in figure 6.6 corresponds (roughly) to an equal increment in loudness. The differences in power vary immensely. But when these differences are stated in decibels, each step is seen to be the same. By means of the decibel system, not only are the awkward numbers involved reduced to manageable proportions, but also differences in power between sounds are stated in a way which corresponds very nearly with our ideas of loudness. There is at the most a 10% error involved in equating our impressions of differences in loudness with the actual differences in decibels between sounds.

Of course, the rule we have given for finding the common logarithm of a number applies only to figures of the form 10, or 100, or 1,000, etc. When the power ratio between two sounds is some intermediate value, such as 1 to 4, we have to use logarithm tables as a step in finding the differences in decibels between the sounds. Table 6.3 gives you some idea of a few of these intermediate values. In the earlier part of this book we talked about the amplitudes of sounds rather than their powers; accordingly, a column showing the amplitude ratios is also included.

The values given in the first row of table 6.3 are of particular interest. They show that when the power of one sound is half that of another, the amplitude of the first sound is 0.707 times that of the second (since the power depends on the square of the amplitude, and 0.707 squared equals 0.5, i.e., one-half). As you can see, under these circumstances the log of the power ratio is 0.3, so that the one sound is 3 dB below the other. These values are important because, as we saw in the previous chapter, we usually consider the effective bandwidth of a resonator to be the range over which a resonator will respond to a level input in such a way that all the frequencies within this range have an amplitude of at least 70.7% of the largest amplitude. Now that the connection between amplitude and power has been explained, we can see how the value 70.7% arises; all the frequencies within this range have at least half the power of the maximum output. Accordingly, this measure of the effective range of a resonator is often known as the half-power band-

Table 6.3 Power Ratios and Amplitude Ratios

Power Ratio	Amplitude Ratio	Log of the Power Ratio	Difference in Decibels
0.5 (or 1 to 2)	0.707	0.3	3
0.25 (or 1 to 4)	0.50	0.6	6
0.10 (or 1 to 10)	0.32	1.0	10

width. We measure the bandwidth of a resonator or a filter by noting the frequencies that are 3 dB below the frequency with the maximum amplitude.

At the beginning of the section on amplitude and power we said that the reference sound was almost as loud as the softest sound that the ear could just detect under suitable experimental conditions. In fact the power that a sound has to have before we can hear it depends on the frequency of the sound. We can hear notes in the middle of the frequency range when they are only a little more powerful than the reference sound; but very low notes or very high notes have to be far more powerful before we can hear them. The lower curve in figure 6.7 shows the range of values applicable to a young person with normal hearing. As you can see, when a tone with a frequency of 125 Hz is just audible, it is 30 dB more powerful than the just audible note with a frequency of 2,000 Hz. In other words, the ear is more efficient in the middle of its range. It takes a good deal more power to make it work for either very low notes or very high notes. Once

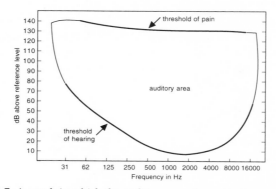

Fig. 6.7. A graph in which the auditory area shows the frequency and amplitude limits of all audible tones.

we get beyond certain frequency limits, there cannot be a sensation of sound, no matter how great the power of the disturbance in the air may be. This is because part of the hearing mechanism cannot be made to vibrate at these extremely high or low frequencies.

The upper line in figure 6.7 represents the level at which the sounds begin to cause a feeling of pain in the ear. If the power of a sound of almost any frequency is raised until it is 130 dB above the reference level, then there will be a feeling of discomfort. Accordingly, figure 6.7 shows the total extent of possible auditory sensations; all audible variations in air pressure must have frequencies and amplitudes that lie within the ranges indicated.

So far in this chapter we have said nothing about differences in quality among sounds. This is largely because we can usually discuss the quality of a sound in terms of the frequencies and amplitudes of its components, i.e., in terms of its spectrum. There are, however, one or two additional factors that we must take into account. The most important of these is a phenomenon which is known as masking. One sound is said to be masked by a second sound when it cannot be heard because of the presence of the other sound. Most of the work on this topic has been done using pure tones or noise rather than complex sounds such as those of speech. But the work that has been done shows that if, for instance, the amplitude of a pure tone with a frequency of 3,500 Hz is 40 dB below the amplitude of a tone with a frequency of 2,500 Hz, then the 3,500 Hz tone will not be heard because it is masked by the other tone. This kind of work is very important in our consideration of the perception of speech sounds. It shows that in a sound such as that shown in figure 6.8, the peak marked with an arrow is insignificant

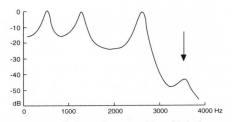

Fig. 6.8. The spectrum of a complex sound in which the components in the peak marked with an arrow are masked by the other components with greater amplitude.

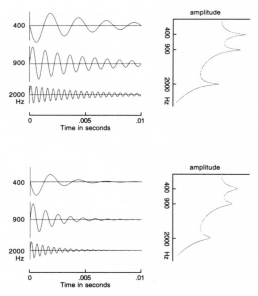

Fig. 6.9. Two sounds each composed of three damped waves. The peaks in the spectrum of the sound in the lower part of the figure are broader than those of the sound in the upper part of the figure, and the components in the lower part of the figure are correspondingly more highly damped. There is very little auditory difference between these two sounds.

from the listener's point of view because it cannot be heard in the presence of the other components with greater amplitudes.

Further research is needed in connection with our perception of damped waveforms, which, as we will see in the next chapter, are very important in the consideration of speech sounds. There is much that we do not know about the effect of different degrees of damping. There is every indication that there is very little apparent difference between a sound consisting of three lightly damped waves as in the upper part of figure 6.9 and the sound composed of three heavily damped waves shown immediately below it. But it is not possible to say much about the limits of this phenomenon at the moment.

CHAPTER SEVEN

The Production of Speech

When we talk we use our tongues and lips and other vocal organs to produce the different speech sounds. In this chapter we will consider the variations in air pressure that are peculiar to each speech sound. It is not within the scope of this book to give a detailed explanation of all the various sounds of speech. We will simply examine some of the main types of sounds that occur in English.

In chapter 1 I pointed out that for every sound there must be a corresponding movement of a source of sound. In the majority of speech sounds the vibrations of the air in the passages of the mouth, throat, and nose (which are collectively known as the vocal tract) serve as the movements that initiate the sound waves. The vocal tract is terminated at one end by the vocal folds and at the other is open to the air beyond the lips and nostrils; thus it forms a resonating chamber of a complex shape. When the air in this chamber is set in motion by a sharp tap, it vibrates in a complex way. It is these vibrations that cause the sound waves which we hear.

The taps that set the air in the mouth and throat in vibration are due to the actions of the vocal cords. The vocal folds are small folds of muscle supported by cartilages in the larynx. In speech or singing they are brought loosely together. If air is being pushed out of the lungs, pressure will be built up beneath them until they are blown apart. But as soon as they have been blown apart, there is less pressure beneath them, and they come together again— which results in the pressure being built up so that they are blown apart again. This cycle of events is repeated very rapidly until air is no longer being pushed out of the lungs or the position of the vocal folds is adjusted. The rush of air between the vocal folds actually causes them to be sucked together, so that they close very sharply. The abrupt change in air pressure that occurs when the vocal folds come together acts like a blow on the air in the vocal tract and sets it vibrating.

The air in the vocal tract will vibrate in different ways when the vocal organs are in different positions. As we saw in chapter 5, the way in which a body of air vibrates depends on its size and shape. The variations in the shape of the vocal tract are determined largely by the movements of the tongue, the lips, and the soft palate. There will be a characteristic mode of vibration of the air corresponding to each position of these vocal organs.

We can now see how the waveforms of the vowel sounds which we discussed in chapter 3 were generated. The waveform of the vowel [ɔ] as in *caught* is repeated here in figure 7.1. As we have already noted, it consists of a series of damped waves, recurring on this occasion at the rate of about 100 per second. Each of these damped waves is produced by the vibrations of the air in the vocal tract which recur every time there is a pulse from the vocal cords. As long as the vocal organs are in the positions for this vowel, and the vocal folds continue producing pulses, a series of damped waves with a frequency of about 500 Hz will be generated.

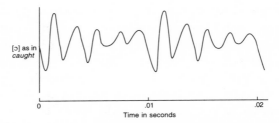

Fig. 7.1. The waveform produced when the author pronounced the vowel [ɔ] as in *caught*.

When the vocal organs take up another position, such as that for the vowel [i] in *see,* another series of damped waves is produced. As we can see from figure 7.2, which is a repetition of another part of figure 3.3, the waveform has at least two principal components that are distinguishable by eye. In fact it would be better to consider the waveform for [i] as in *see* as being more like the sum of three damped waves; and even this is a simplification, as there are some additional smaller components.

Damped waves with appropriate frequencies are shown in figure 7.3. Every time there is a pulse from the vocal cords, the air in the mouth and throat is set vibrating in all three of these ways simultaneously. The figure shows what might result from two such pulses. The sound [i] is the sum of all these vibrations and has components in its spectrum at corresponding frequencies.

The peaks in the spectra of vowels (and as we shall see, of certain other speech sounds as well) correspond to the basic frequencies of the vibrations of the air in the vocal tract. These modes of vibration of the vocal tract are known as formants. The formants of a sound are thus aspects of it that are directly dependent on the shape of the vocal tract and are largely responsible for the characteris-

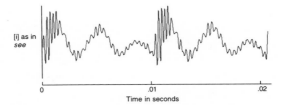

Fig. 7.2. The waveform produced when the author pronounced the vowel [i] as in *see*.

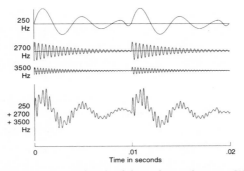

Fig. 7.3. Two repetitions of each of three damped waves. When these three waveforms are added together they produce a sound wave somewhat like that of [i] as in *see*.

tic quality. The author's vowel [ɔ] is partly characterized by a formant around 500 Hz, and his vowel [i] by formants around 250, 2,700, and 3,500 Hz. When these vowels are pronounced there will be comparatively large components corresponding to the damped waves with these basic frequencies. It is the presence of these distinctive components (these formants) that enables us to recognize the different vowels that are associated with the different positions of the vocal organs.

Each movement of the vocal folds sets the body of air above them vibrating at its own natural frequencies (the formant frequencies). If the vocal folds are blown apart every hundredth of a second, the damped vibrations will be initiated a hundred times per second, and the complex waveform which is produced beyond the lips will be repeated at the same rate. This point is illustrated in figure 7.4, which shows the sound waves corresponding to a synthesized sound that has a slightly simpler waveform but is almost indistinguishable from the vowel [ɔ] as in *caught*. Four different situations are shown: (*a*) the result of a single pulse, (*b*) the result of pulses recurring every hundredth of a second, and (*c*) and (*d*) the result of pulses at two other rates. A speech synthesizer was used to produce the sounds for these diagrams so as to ensure that the only difference between the sounds was the rate at which the pulses were produced.

We saw in chapter 4 that repetitive waveforms such as that in figure 7.4(*b*) can be conveniently regarded as being the sum of a number of components, each of which has a frequency that is a whole-number multiple of the fundamental frequency (i.e., the frequency of repetition of the complex wave). Thus the wave in figure 7.4(*b*) will have components that are whole number multiples of 100, since this complex wave is repeated 100 times per second. In fact the spectrum of this sound is as shown on the right of figure 7.4. The component with a frequency of 500 Hz has the largest amplitude (which is not surprising, as the damped wave that is repeated has a basic frequency of 500 Hz). In addition there is another peak in the spectrum at 1,500 Hz that corresponds to the smaller waves superimposed on the main damped waveform. In (*c*) and (*d*) of figure 7.4 are the waveforms and spectra of the same vowel-like sound on a higher pitch, i.e., when

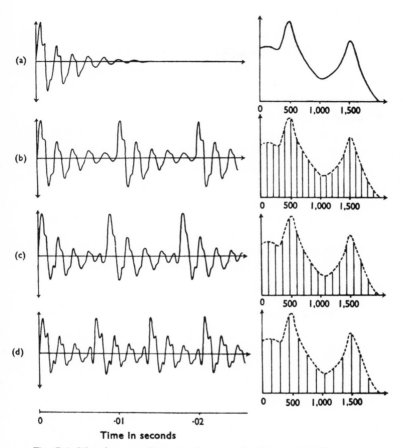

Fig. 7.4. Waveforms and spectra for a synthetic vowel similar to the vowel [ɔ] as in *caught*. (*a*) Effect of a single pulse on the resonating system; (*b*) pulses recurring at the rate of 100 a second; (*c*) 120 pulses a second; (*d*) 150 pulses a second.

the pulses are being produced at 120 and 150 Hz. As you can see, these waves all consist of repetitions of a damped wave with a basic frequency of 500-Hz and another wave with a basic frequency of about 1,500 Hz. Furthermore, all the spectra shown on the right of the figure have a certain similarity to one another; it is possible to draw a curve with peaks at 500 and 1,500 Hz around all of them. The difference between these last two spectra is that the component frequencies are multiples in the one case of 120, and in the other of 150; and hence they are represented by lines which are farther apart.

This analysis is, of course, in accordance with the principle stated in chapter 4: when a complex wave consists of a damped waveform repeated at regular intervals, the component frequencies will always have the same relative amplitudes as the corresponding components in the continuous spectrum representing the isolated occurrence of the damped wave. Consequently, altering the rate at which the vocal folds produce pulses will affect the fundamental frequency of the complex wave; but it will not alter the formants (the peaks in the spectrum), which correspond to the basic frequencies of the damped vibrations of the air in the vocal tract. It is in this sense that we may say that the formants of a sound are properties of the corresponding mouth shape.

Since a continuous curve as in figure 7.4(a) is the clearest way of representing the formants which characterize a given vowel irrespective of the rate at which pulses are produced by the vocal cords, we often use it in preference to a line spectrum when we are discussing the acoustic nature of vowel quality. We describe a vowel in terms of line spectra (as in figure 7.4[b], [c], and [d]) only when we want to draw attention to the particular fundamental frequencies employed.

We saw in chapter 6 that the pitch of a sound depends

mainly on the fundamental frequency. Accordingly, when there is a variation in the rate at which pulses are produced by the vocal cords, there will be a change in the pitch of the sound (although there will be no change in the formants, and hence no change in the characteristic vowel quality). We control changes in pitch by adjusting the muscles that act upon the cords. When the tension is increased so that the folds are stretched tightly, they move more rapidly, and so produce the greater number of pulses per second that are required for a high-pitched sound. On the other hand, when we say a word on a low pitch, the folds are held together only loosely, so that when they have been blown apart they take somewhat longer to return to the closed position.

It is usually possible to alter the pitch of a vowel sound without altering its characteristic quality, because each of these factors is controlled by a separate physiological mechanism. As we have seen, the pitch depends on the action of the vocal cords, and the characteristic quality depends largely on the formants, which have certain fixed values for each particular shape of the vocal tract. Figure 7.5 shows the spectra of the author's vowels in the middle parts of the words *heed, hid, head, had, hod, hawed, hood,* and *who'd.* The corresponding positions of the vocal organs are also shown. These curves give a very good indication of the frequency components which are characteristic of each of these sounds. We may think of each peak as showing the basic frequency of one of the damped waves which are present. The vowel in the middle part of the word *had,* for instance, is characterized by having components with relatively large amplitudes in three main regions: around 700 Hz, 1,750 Hz, and 2,600 Hz. Damped waves with these basic frequencies are generated every time there is a pulse from the vocal cords.

If you like to think of it in musical terms, you can say

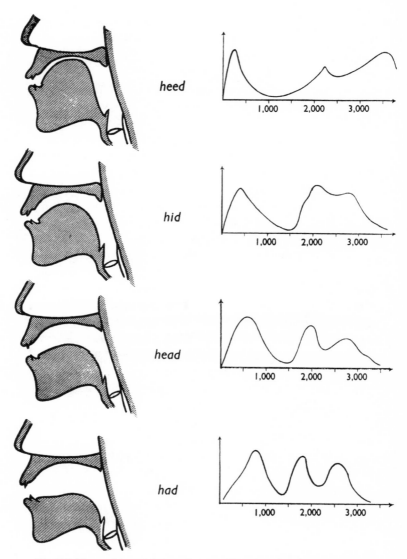

Fig. 7.5. The position of the vocal organs (based on data from X-ray photographs of the author) and the spectra of the vowel sounds in the mid-

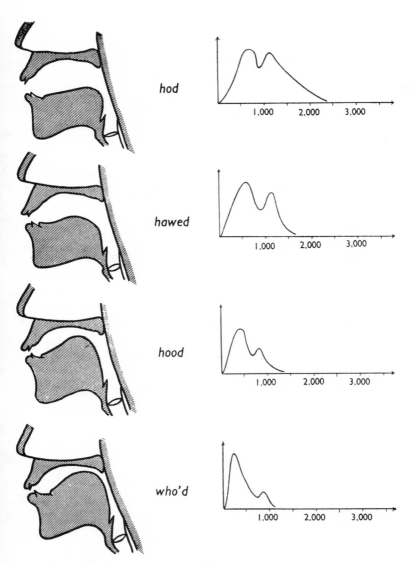

dle of the words *heed, hid, head, had, hod, hawed, hood, who'd*, in the author's speech.

that corresponding to each vowel there is a chord that is characteristic of that vowel. Owing to the pulses from the larynx, this chord is generated many times per second. There is nothing particularly new about this way of looking at speech sounds. As long ago as 1829, Robert Willis said: "A given vowel is merely the rapid repetition of its peculiar note." This is an oversimplification, because Willis did not realize that vowels are characterized not by one frequency each but by a combination of frequencies; if we alter his remark slightly, however, and say that a given vowel is merely the rapid repetition of its peculiar chord, we have a statement that fits the data of figure 7.5 very nicely.

The description of the production of vowel sounds that we have been giving has the merit of being fairly straightforward, but it is not completely satisfactory, in that it does not take into account the nature of the vocal cord pulses. We have been viewing the vocal tract as containing a resonating body of air that is set in motion by a series of sharp taps from the vocal cords. In fact, the pulses produced by the vocal folds are not completely sharp taps. They are variations in air pressure with a waveform, as shown in figure 7.6. If you were able to cut somebody's head off while they were producing a vowel, *and* if they

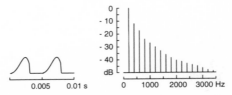

Fig. 7.6. The waveform and spectrum of a typical glottal pulse with a fundamental frequency of 200 Hz.

were able to go on phonating, the sound that they produced would have the waveform shown in this figure.

The spectrum of this waveform is shown on the right of the figure. The wave on the left has two repetitions within 1/100 of a second, so the vocal folds were vibrating at 200 Hz. Consequently all the components in the spectrum on the right are multiples of 200 Hz. We will take the fundamental frequency—the 200 Hz component—as a reference value, and arbitrarily assign it a value of 0 dB. The amplitudes of the other components decrease very rapidly as the frequency increases. The 400 Hz component has an amplitude 12 dB smaller than the 200 Hz component, and the 800 Hz component has an amplitude 12 dB smaller than the 400 Hz component. In fact, the amplitude goes down 12 dB for each doubling of the frequency—the 2,000 Hz component is 12 dB below the 1,000 Hz component. We saw in chapter 2 that any doubling of the frequency is an increase of an octave: standard pitch A on a piano is 440 Hz; the A above it is 880 Hz; and the A above that is 1,760 Hz. We can say that the spectrum of the glottal pulse has a slope of −12 dB per octave. The slope is a negative number because the amplitude goes down by 12 dB for every octave that the frequency goes up.

These considerations lead us to another well-known way of describing the production of vowel sounds. This is in terms of what has been called the source-filter theory. This theory regards the vibrating vocal folds as the source of a wave which is affected by having to pass through a filter formed by the resonating cavities that make up the vocal tract. Instead of viewing the vocal tract as containing a resonating body of air excited by taps from the vocal cords, we will view it as a filter that passes some frequencies better than others. Of course, the frequencies it passes are exactly those at which it will itself resonate. Consequently the curve showing the resonances of the vocal tract is also the curve that shows the extent to which it will pass on frequencies that are put into it.

Figure 7.7 shows a source-filter view of the production of a vowel. The spectrum of the glottal pulse is shown on the left of the figure. In this case we have taken the vocal folds to be vibrating at 100 Hz, so the components are at 100 Hz intervals. To the right of the spectrum is the set of curves specifying the vocal tract response. The output of the vocal tract can be regarded as the input to another box entitled "radiation factor," which we must now take into account. So far we have been considering only the vibrating air inside the vocal tract. But these vibrations are inside the mouth and are not themselves the variations in air pressure that we hear. The air in the vocal tract vibrates so that the air particles at the open end between the lips move backward and forward. It is these movements that start the air outside the lips vibrating. The air between the lips acts like a piston, a source of sound producing variations in air pressure that radiate out from the lips just as the variations in air pressure radiate out from a source of sound such as a tuning fork. The movements of this piston of air are more effective in causing variations in pressure in the surrounding air at some frequencies

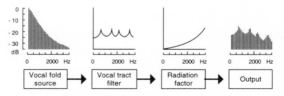

Fig. 7.7. A source-filter view of the production of a vowel.

than others. The higher the frequency, the greater the response of the surrounding air to the action of the air vibrating in the vocal tract. This effect, which we have termed the "radiation factor" ("radiation impedance" is the term used in more technical books), can be regarded as a kind of filter that boosts the higher frequencies by 6 dB per octave. The curve representing the radiation factor is shown above the third box in figure 7.7.

The output produced at the lips depends on the vocal cord source, the filtering action of the vocal tract, and the further modifications produced by the radiation factor. Normally the vocal cord source is the same for each vowel, apart from variations of pitch. The vocal folds may be vibrating at 100 Hz, or at 200 Hz, as in the examples we have been considering, or at any other frequency in the range of the human voice. But irrespective of the fundamental frequency, the spectral slope of the cord pulse will usually be approximately -12 dB per octave. The filtering action of the vocal tract will be different for each position of the vocal organs, thus producing formants (peaks in the resonance curve) at different frequencies. The spectrum of the waveform beyond the lips (shown on the right of figure 7.7) will have peaks in regions which depend on the filter characteristics of the vocal tract. The general slope of the output spectrum will be influenced by the slope of the spectrum of the glottal pulse (-12 dB/octave) and the radiation factor ($+6$ dB/octave). Taken together these two slope factors account for a -6 dB/octave slope in the output spectrum. The major characteristics of the output spectrum—the formant peaks—are superimposed on this general slope. They are primarily dependent on the filtering characteristics of the vocal tract.

As vowels are characterized to such an extent by the

frequencies of their formants, it is often convenient to represent them by a diagram (figure 7.8) which shows only this information. This diagram, which is based on the data shown in figure 7.5, uses the vertical scale to indicate the frequencies of the formants that characterize the various vowels. Diagrams similar to this, called spectrograms, are often produced in acoustic analyses of speech. The horizontal scale (the abscissa) indicates the time at which a certain sound occurred; the vertical scale indicates the component frequencies that are present at the times shown on the horizontal scale; and the lightness or darkness of the marking indicates the amplitudes of the various components.

Figure 7.8 is one of the basic diagrams in the study of the acoustics of speech. We can verify some of the data without using any instruments. It is, for instance, pos-

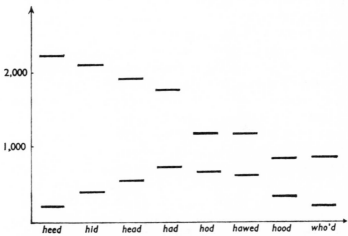

Fig. 7.8. A schematic spectrogram showing the frequencies of the first and second formants of some of the English vowels as pronounced by the author.

sible to set the air in the vocal tract vibrating in such a way that the damped wave corresponding to the lowest formant is produced with a greater amplitude than the other components. This can be done by flicking a finger against the throat just above the larynx while holding the breath by means of a glottal stop (the sound often replacing [t] in the word *button*). When you do this a dull hollow note is produced. This sound is composed mainly of a damped wave with a basic frequency corresponding to that of the first formant.

If you look at figure 7.8 you will see that the first formant (i.e., the lowest peak in the spectrum) is at a low frequency for the word *heed* (220 Hz), and is a little higher for each of the words *hid* (400 Hz), *head* (550 Hz), and *had* (750 Hz). If you place your vocal organs in the positions for making the vowels in each of these words and then flick your finger against your throat while holding a glottal stop, you will produce a low-pitched note for the word *heed* and a slightly higher one for each of the words *hid*, *head*, and *had*. In the remaining words in this series the frequency of the first formant descends. Consequently, if you repeat this trick while making the articulations for the vowels in the words *hod*, *hawed*, *hood*, and *who'd*, you will produce a series of notes that descend in pitch. The actual frequencies of the notes you produce may, of course, differ from those quoted above, which are round values based on an analysis of the author's speech. You may have not only a different accent but also a larger or smaller vocal tract. Both these features will affect the absolute values of the formant frequencies, but they will probably not affect the relative arrangement of the sounds you produce.

We can make a rough check on the frequency of the second formant for each of these vowels by whispering the words. When you whisper, the vocal folds are held slightly apart, so that the air from the lungs rushes through them, causing small variations in air pressure that will set the air in the vocal tract vibrating. Among the basic frequencies that are often the most clearly audible under these conditions are those of the second and higher formants. If you whisper the set of words *heed, hid, head, had, hod, hawed, hood, who'd* you will hear a gradual lowering of the apparent pitch. As you can see from figure 7.7, this is paralleled by the way in which the second formant becomes progressively lower for each of the vowels in this series. It should be noted, however, that this is a very rough method of checking one of the basic frequencies associated with a vowel. When we whisper each of the first four words in the series *heed, hid,* etc., the pitch of the whispered sound probably does correspond more or less to the frequency of the second formant; but for the last four words, when the two formants are fairly close together, and the amplitude of the lowest one is relatively greater, the whisper pitch may correspond more to the first formant than to the second.

In the next chapter we will consider in more detail the relationships between the formant frequencies and the shapes of the vocal tract. Here we will note some general tendencies that can be seen by comparing the diagrams of the vocal tract shown in figure 7.5 with the corresponding spectra. In general, formant frequencies depend on three factors: the position of the point of maximum constriction in the vocal tract (which is controlled by the backward and forward movement of the tongue), the size or cross-sectional area of the maximum constriction (which is controlled by the movements of the tongue toward and away from the roof of the mouth and the back of the throat), and the position of the lips.

For vowels such as those in *heed, hid, head,* and *had,* the chief cause of the variation in the frequency of the first formant is the variation in the size of the maximum constriction in the vocal tract. The tongue is closest to the roof of the mouth for the word *heed;* and for each of the other words, it is a little less close. As a rough rule we can say that for vowels of this sort, as the cross-sectional area of the maximum constriction of the vocal tract increases, the frequency of the lowest formant also increases. For vowels such as those in *hod, hawed, hood,* and *who'd,* the variation in the frequency of the first formant is determined largely by the position of the point of maximum constriction. In these vowels the constriction is in the pharynx or the back of the mouth, and during this series it moves progressively forward. As the point of maximum constriction moves further from the glottis, the size of the body of air behind the constriction becomes larger and the frequency of the first formant decreases.

The variation in the frequency of the second formant in the vowels in the words *heed, hid, head,* and *had* also depends mainly on the variation in the size of the maximum constriction in the vocal tract. But the rule is the reverse of that applicable to the first formant. As the constriction increases, the frequency of the second formant decreases. Variations in the second formant frequency are also due to the rounding of the lips. However, this movement will cause in addition a decrease in the amplitude of the second and higher peaks. In the series of words *heed, hid, head, had, hod, hawed, hood, who'd,* the lips become progressively more rounded. In the last four of these words it is the movement of the lips rather than the movement of the tongue which results in the lowering of the frequency of the second resonance peak. Note that the increase in lip rounding also accounts for the decrease in the relative amplitudes of the second and third peaks in the last four words of the series.

Many other sounds of speech are formed in a similar way to the vowels we have been describing. For example, nasal sounds, such as those at the ends of the words *ram*, *ran*, and *rang*, and laterals, such as those at the beginnings and ends of the words *little* and *lull*, also depend on pulses from the vocal folds setting the air in the vocal tract in vibration. For each of these sounds there are characteristic positions of the vocal organs, and consequently a particular resonance curve can be associated with each of them. During the pronunciation of the last sound in the word *ram*, for instance, the vocal organs are in the positions shown in figure 7.9. The lips are closed, but the air passage through the nose is open. This particular shape of the vocal tract has a resonance curve as shown in figure 7.10. The largest damped waves which are typical of this sound have basic frequencies of about 220 Hz and 2,500

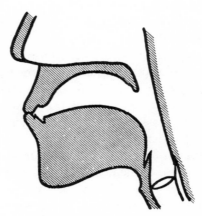

Fig. 7.9. The position of the vocal organs during the [m] in *ram*.

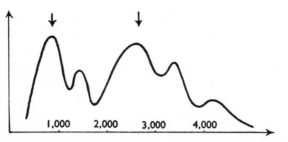

Fig. 7.10. The resonance curve of the vocal tract during the pronunciation of the last sound in the word *ram*.

Hz. Each of the nasal sounds is characterized by a large
low-frequency component.

In the English vowels, nasals, and laterals, the main
source of acoustic energy is the production of pulses by
the vocal cords. But the stream of breath from the lungs
can be used to form sounds in other ways. A typical
speech sound in which the vocal folds are not in action
occurs at the beginning of the word *sip*. When we say this
word we begin by raising the tongue so that it is close behind the upper front teeth, forming a very narrow gap
through which the air from the lungs is forced. The jet of
air formed by this groove in the tongue strikes the edges
of the teeth with a high velocity. As a result of this there
are many small semirandom variations in air pressure
which, taken together, constitute the high-frequency hissing noise that we associate with [s]. Similar nonrepetitive wave forms occur in the pronunciation of the
voiceless sounds [ʃ, θ, f], as in *shin, thin,* and *fin.*

Some speech sounds are formed by a combination of
the two mechanisms that we have discussed so far. Thus
the sound at the beginning of the word *zoo*, for instance,
is the result of setting the air in the vocal tract vibrating by
means of pulses from the vocal cords and at the same

time generating additional variations in air pressure by forcing air through a narrow channel as in the production of an [s] sound. The sounds at the beginnings of the words *vat* and *that* are also formed by a combination of these two acoustic mechanisms.

One of the other sounds of English which it is interesting to discuss is the sound which is usually written with the letter *h*. In this sound the vocal folds are not in action as they are when we say a vowel; nor is there any acoustic energy generated by forcing air through a narrow gap. Instead the air from the lungs has a relatively free passage out through the vocal tract. But whenever an airstream passes through the vocal cavities, some small variations in air pressure will be caused by the irregular surfaces which obstruct the flow; and these pressure variations will be sufficient to produce very slight vibrations of the body of air in the vocal tract. As the positions of the articulators during the sound [h] are similar to those of the surrounding sounds, such as the adjacent vowels, the frequency components in [h] sounds have relative amplitudes similar to those in vowels; but the complex wave has a smaller amplitude and no fundamental frequency, as it is not generated by regular pulses from the vocal cords.

So far we have not discussed an important set of sounds, those at the beginnings and ends of the words *pip, bib, tit, did, kick,* and *gig.* Of course the consonants in these words should be thought of not as sounds in themselves but as ways of beginning and ending the vowels. Each of them involves an abrupt change in the wave form associated with the vowel.

The consonants in the words *pip, tit,* and *kick* are distinguished from those in *bib, did,* and *gig* by the action of the vocal cords. In the latter group the vocal folds begin generating pulses earlier in the articulation of each word and continue doing so for longer than in the first group. Within each group the words are partly distinguished from one another by differences in the shape of the vocal tract. During the word *gig,* for instance, the tongue is at no time in any of the positions that it passes through during the pronunciation of the word *did.* (If you want to check this, try saying a sentence such as *"Did* he get his *gig?"* You will probably find that at no time during the first word is the tip of the tongue behind the lower front teeth, where it is throughout the last word; and during all of the last word the back of the tongue is raised toward the soft palate, whereas in the first word it is relatively flat in the mouth.) These differences in the shape of the vocal tract affect the vowels in each of these words; and the shape of the vocal tract as it moves to or from a position for a consonant closure also results in the accompanying sounds having characteristic qualities. We associate these different qualities with the different consonants at the beginnings and ends of these words.

CHAPTER EIGHT
Resonances of the Vocal Tract

In the previous chapter we described the acoustic structure of some speech sounds. We must now explain how these particular resonances of the vocal tract arise. In order to do this we have to reexamine how air vibrates when sound waves are produced. We know that each particle of air moves backward and forward, passing its vibrations on to the particles next to it. We also know that sound takes time to travel. If you see the flash of a gun which is a mile away, it will be four or five seconds before you hear the sound of the explosion. Sound travels in air at about 350 meters per second (depending slightly on the temperature and the amount of moisture in the air). Now consider a source of sound that is vibrating at 350 Hz. After one second the air 350 meters away will also be vibrating at that rate (assuming the source of sound is loud enough). We will therefore have a situation as shown diagramatically in figure 8.1. Because the source of sound is vibrating at 350 Hz, after one second there will be 350 peaks of pressure spaced over 350 meters. In other words, the peaks of pressure will be one meter apart. If the source of sound had been vibrating at 700 Hz, there would have been twice as many peaks within the distance that sound travels within one second, so the

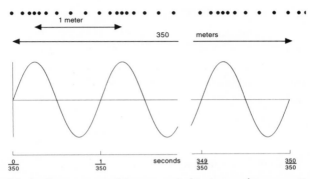

Fig. 8.1. At the top a sound is represented in terms of movements of particles of air produced by a source of sound vibrating at 350 Hz. The diagram below shows that peaks of air pressure are one meter apart, as there are 350 peaks in 350 meters, which is the distance sound travels in one second.

peaks would have to be closer together; they would have been 350/700 = 0.5 meter apart.

The distance between the peaks of pressure is called the wavelength of the sound. As you can see from the examples discussed in the previous paragraph, the wavelength depends on the frequency. For a sound with a frequency of 350 Hz, the wavelength will be 1 meter; for a sound with a higher frequency it will be shorter, as more waves have to occur within the same distance; for a low-pitched sound it will be longer. If the speed of sound is considered to be 350 meters per second, we can express this relationship in the form of an equation:

frequency (in Hz) times wavelength (in meters) = 350.

For our purposes it is more useful to think in terms of centimeters rather than meters, so we can write:

$$f\lambda = c = 35,000$$

where f is the frequency, λ (the Greek symbol lambda) is the wavelength, and c is the speed of sound, which, for simplicity, we will take to be 35,000 cm per second. If (as is often the case) we know the wavelength of a sound and want to determine its frequency, we can rearrange this equation and say:

$$f = c/\lambda = 35,000/\lambda.$$

Taking this equation, we can see that if a sound has a very long wavelength, say 10 meters, then it has a very low frequency, namely, $35,000/1,000 = 35$ Hz. Conversely, if it has a very short wavelength, say 2 cm, then it will have a high frequency of $35,000/2 = 17,500$ Hz. Both these sounds are near the limits of hearing, in part because these wavelengths are near the extremes that can be fitted into a normal human environment.

Now let us return to the production of speech sounds. We will begin by considering the simple case of a neutral vocal tract in the position for the vowel [ə], as at the end of the word *sofa*. We will take the vocal tract to be a tube about 17.5 cm long (it is actually slightly less for most speakers, but this is a convenient figure because it keeps the arithmetic simple). The vocal tract can be considered to be closed at one end by the vibrating vocal cords and to have an opening at the other end formed by the lips. (Even when the vibrating vocal cords are apart, the distance between them is comparatively small, and we can still consider the tube to be closed at one end.) During the vowel [ə] there are no significant constrictions, and we will regard the tube as having a uniform diameter of about 1 cm. We have therefore taken a complex tube with a shape as shown on the left of figure 8.2 and regarded it as if it were the simpler tube shown on the right. We must

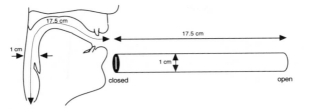

Fig. 8.2. A schematic diagram of a neutral vocal tract in the position for the vowel [ə] on the left, and a simplified version of that shape as a tube closed at one end on the right.

now see how the air in such a tube will vibrate in response to the complex wave produced at its input by the vocal cords.

We saw in the last chapter that the complex wave at the glottis has component frequencies extending up to at least 4,000 Hz with considerable amplitude. Some of these component frequencies will be similar to the natural frequencies of vibration of the body of air contained within the vocal tract. These components will thus be able to give the air in the tract appropriately timed small pushes so that it is able to build up large vibrations, just as small appropriately timed pushes on a swing produce large movements. A more direct analogy to the production of movements of air in the vocal tract can be observed by considering what happens when you blow across the neck of a bottle. The rapid stream of air passing over the mouth of the bottle is set vibrating at a wide range of frequencies. Some of these frequencies will be similar to the natural frequencies of vibration of the air in the bottle. These particular frequencies will set the air in the bottle in motion, so that after a very short time, there will be relatively large movements. The air in the bottle will move in and out of the neck of the bottle in a regular way, having an effect much like a moving piston, or the diaphragm of a loudspeaker, itself acting as a source of sound. Thus the small vibrations in the air that is being blown across the neck of the bottle build up much larger vibrations at a particular frequency. As you can tell from blowing across bottles of different shapes and sizes, the frequency depends on the shape and size of the enclosed body of air. Our task now is to determine the frequencies at which the body of air in the vocal tract will prefer to vibrate.

We will continue considering the simplest possible vocal tract shape (which we are taking to be even simpler than it really is), a tube closed at one end and about 17.5 cm long. If a tube is closed at one end, the particles of air at that end cannot move back and forth. At the open end, however, they will be unconstrained and can have their maximum movement. The air in a tube behaves like a spring, being alternately compressed and expanded, with the air at the open end moving most and the air near the glottis moving least. Figure 8.3 shows (in a rather exaggerated form) two views of the air, the first, at the top of the picture, when it is maximally expanded, and the second, just below, when it is maximally compressed. In order to produce these expansions and contractions, the particles of air may move fast or slowly. We can draw a graph of this movement of the air, showing the maximum rate of flow of the air particles in different parts of the tube, as in the lower left of figure 8.3. The maximum flow is at the open end, the minimum (in fact, zero) flow, at the closed end. As a result of these movements of air particles, there are changes in the air pressure within the tube. The pressure is maximal at the closed end, where the particles are all pushed together, and zero at the end which is open to the surrounding air, as shown in the graph at the lower right.

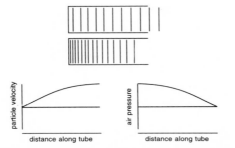

Fig. 8.3. The air in a tube vibrating like a spring, at the top when the spring is maximally expanded, and just below when it is maximally contracted. At the bottom left is a graph of the rate of flow of air in each part of the tube, and at the right, a graph of the maximum pressure at each point.

If we think of these air flow and pressure changes as being part of a sound wave, we can see what the wavelength would be. Figure 8.4 takes the particle velocity wave of figure 8.3 (we could have taken the pressure wave form equally well) and extends it so that the complete wave can be seen. It is apparent that this variation in air flow (or air pressure) has a wavelength that is four times as long as the length of the tube.

Knowing the wavelength, we can use the equation we discussed above to determine the frequency of vibration of this spring of air. We took the tube representing the vocal tract to be 17.5 cm long. The wavelength is therefore four times 17.5, i.e., 70 cm. It follows that the frequency at which this body of air is vibrating $= c/\lambda = 35,000/70 = 500$ Hz. We can therefore say that a wave of 500 Hz corresponds to one of the modes of vibration of the air in a vocal tract when it is in the position for a neutral vowel.

The diagram in figure 8.3 shows one way in which air can vibrate in a tube that is closed at one end and open at the other. This is not, however, the only way in which the

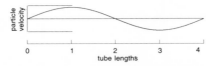

Fig. 8.4. The graph showing particle velocity in fig. 8.3 extended so as to form a complete variation in air flow.

air in a tube of this sort can vibrate. The only constraint on the movement of the air particles is that they should be free to move at a maximum velocity at the open end, and there should be no movement at the closed end. There can be more complex variations in the middle of the tube. Another wave which fits in with the constraints at the ends of the tube but has additional variations else-where is shown in figure 8.5. There is maximal move-ment not only at the open end but also at points within the tube; and there is minimum movement (correspond-ing to high pressure) not only at the closed end but also elsewhere. As you can see, if we consider the cycle as the whole wave, part of it is within the tube, and part is out-side it. If we divide the tube into thirds, as shown by the dashed lines, it is as if we needed an extra one-third to make up a complete cycle of this wave. In other words, the wavelength is four-thirds of the tube length. If we say that the length of the tube is L, then the wavelength is 4 times $L/3$. Consequently the equation for the frequency of this wave is:

$$f = \frac{c}{\lambda} = \frac{35,000}{4\,L/3} = \frac{35,000 * 3}{4 * L} = \frac{35,000 * 3}{70}$$

$$= 500 * 3 = 1,500 \text{ Hz}.$$

There are many more waves that will fit appropriately within this open-ended tube. One of them is shown in

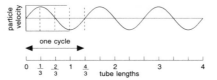

Fig. 8.5. Variations in air flow such that $\frac{3}{4}$ of the wave is within the tube.

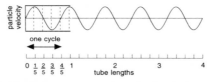

Fig. 8.6. Variations in air flow such that a cycle plus an extra quarter of a cycle, making a total $\frac{5}{4}$ of a cycle, are within the tube.

figure 8.6. In this case more than a complete cycle is within the tube. If you divide the tube into fifths, as shown by the dashed lines, then you can see that only four-fifths are needed for a complete cycle. This wave has a wavelength of 4 times $L/5$, where L is the tube length. Its frequency is therefore:

$$f = \frac{c}{\lambda} = \frac{35{,}000}{4\ L/5} = \frac{35{,}000 * 5}{4 * 17.5} = \frac{35{,}000 * 5}{70}$$

$$= 500 * 5 = 2{,}500 \text{ Hz}.$$

We have now seen that a neutral vocal tract will have one resonance at 500 Hz, another at 1,500 Hz, and a third at 2,500 Hz. These are approximately the formant frequencies of the vowel [ə] as at the end of *sofa*. The first formant corresponds to the lowest resonance, in which a quarter of the wave is within the tube, so that the wavelength is equivalent to four times the vocal tract length.

The second formant is the next-lowest resonance, in which three-quarters of the wave is within the tract; and the third formant is the next resonance, in which five-fourths of the wave are within the tract.

The air in the vocal tract vibrates in all these ways in response to the complex wave produced at the glottis. We can write a general formula for the possible frequencies of vibration in a neutral vocal tract that is closed at one end and open at the other:

$$f = \frac{c * (2n - 1)}{4L}$$

where n is any integer, and L is the length of the vocal tract. If $n = 1$, then, as $(2n - 1) = 1$, we can write:

$$f = \frac{c * 1}{4L} = 500 \text{ Hz}.$$

This is called the quarter wave resonance of the vocal tract. Similarly, we worked out the cases where $n = 2$, and $(2n - 1) = 3$:

$$f = \frac{c * 3}{4L} = 1{,}500 \text{ Hz},$$

which is called the three-quarter wave resonance, and $n = 3$ so that $(2n - 1) = 5$,

$$f = \frac{c * 5}{4L} = 2{,}500 \text{ Hz},$$

which is the five-fourths wave resonance. Continuing these notions, we can see that a neutral vocal tract of 17.5 cm length will have resonances at 500, 1,500, 2,500, 3,500, and 4,500 Hz, and so on indefinitely. In practice we can disregard the resonances above 4,500 Hz, as they will have such a small amplitude (remember that we saw in the previous chapter that the frequencies present in a voiced sound decrease by 6 dB per octave). But if we ask at what frequencies could the air in a (simplified) neutral vocal tract vibrate most easily, given a suitable input, then the answer is that there are resonances every 1,000 Hz, starting from 500 Hz and going up to infinity.

We can apply the same kind of considerations to calculate the resonances that occur in some other vocal tract shapes. The vowel [ɑ] as in *father* has a comparatively open mouth cavity and a tongue that is low and pulled back into the pharynx. As a gross simplification we can consider the vocal tract to consist of two tubes, a narrow one in the pharynx and a larger one in front representing the mouth cavity, as shown in figure 8.7.

The pharynx tube is closed at the glottis, and comparatively open at the end where it joins the tube representing the mouth cavity. The mouth tube is open at the lips, and in comparison with this large opening, we can consider it to be closed at the end in the pharynx. We therefore have a situation in which we have two tubes of

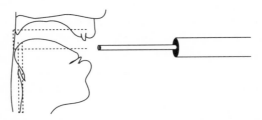

Fig. 8.7. The shape of the vocal tract in the vowel [ɑ] as in *father* schematized as two tubes.

approximately equal length—each about half the length of the vocal tract—and each open at one end and comparatively closed at the other. One tube is much wider than the other, but this is immaterial to the calculation of the resonant frequency, as the wavelength (which determines the frequency) depends only on the length of the tube in the model of the vocal tract that we are considering. This is in fact true as long as the tube is not too wide. For a wave to be considered as traveling only up and down a tube, the width must be less than a quarter of the length. This is the case in a normal vocal tract (although not in the diagrams we have been considering, in which the width has been exaggerated so that the wave can be seen more clearly). As we have seen, the vocal tract is about 17.5 cm long; in the production of vowels its diameter varies from a few millimeters to a maximum of about 3.5 cm.

Because each of the tubes in our model of the vowel [ɑ] is half the length of the vocal tract, their resonant frequencies will be double the resonant frequencies of the tract as a whole. So instead of having resonances at 500, 1,500 Hz, etc., they will in theory be at 1,000, 3,000 Hz, etc. In practice, the mouth tube is not completely closed at one end, and there will be some interaction between the movements of the air particles in this tube and that of the air particles in the pharynx tube. The net effect of this interaction will be that the resonant frequency of the pharynx tube will be slightly lower, and that of the mouth tube slightly higher. The lower resonance will be at about 900 Hz, and the higher at about 1,100 Hz—frequencies that are close to those of the formants in an [ɑ] vowel.

If we think of the vocal tract as consisting of two tubes in this way, we can see that as the tongue moves backward and forward in the mouth, one of the tubes gets shorter and the other gets longer. Figure 8.8 is a graph of the frequencies of the two tubes, assuming that together they have a total length of 17.5 cm. The midpoint in this graph is approximately that corresponding to the vowel [ɑ].

The longer of the two tubes in figure 8.8 will always produce the lowest resonance, and this will be equivalent to the first formant. As the tube gets longer, this resonance will fall. The longest this tube can be is the full length of the vocal tract, which we have taken to be 17.5 cm; and as we have seen, the first resonance of a tube of this kind is 500 Hz. But we saw in the previous chapter that the first formant can have a frequency lower than this—in the vowel [i] as in *see* it may be as low as 250 Hz. We now have to consider how such resonances can arise, and obviously our simple two-tube model will not be appropriate. We can use a two-tube model to explain why a speaker with a vocal tract length of 17.5 cm will always have a first formant below 900 Hz. This is because the longer of the two tubes has the lower resonant frequency, corresponding to the first formant. The shortest that the longer of the two tubes can be is half the vocal tract

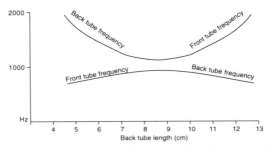

Fig. 8.8. The resonances of two tubes, one being taken as equivalent to part of the vocal tract in the back of the mouth and the pharynx, the other as equivalent to that in the front of the mouth.

length; and this tube cannot produce a resonance higher than 900–1,000 Hz, the resonance of half the vocal tract. But a tube model does not help explain how low first-formant frequencies are produced.

The solution to this problem is to consider the air in the vocal tract not as if it were in a tube open at one end but as if part of it were totally enclosed. On some occasions the part of the vocal tract behind the tongue constriction—the back cavity—behaves more like air vibrating in a bottle when you blow across its neck. This kind of device is known as a Helmholtz resonator. It is an arrangement in which a small body of air, such as that in the neck of a bottle, acts like a piston vibrating back and forth on the spring provided by the larger body of air in the main part of the bottle, as shown in figure 8.9. The rate of vibration—the frequency that is produced—depends partly on the volume of air in the enclosed space and partly on the mass of the air in the neck, which may be thought of as a weight bouncing on a spring.

Part of the vocal tract behaves much like a Helmholtz resonator in the production of a vowel such as [i] as in *see*. In this vowel, the front of the tongue is raised toward the hard palate, forming a narrow channel corresponding to the neck of a bottle. Behind this tongue constriction there is a large body of air in the back of the mouth and the pharynx, which form the body of the bottle. In front there is a short open tube with a resonant frequency determined by its length in the way that we discussed previ-

Fig. 8.9. A Helmholtz resonator in the form of a bottle in which the air in the neck behaves as a mass that can vibrate back and forth on the compressible body of air within the bottle.

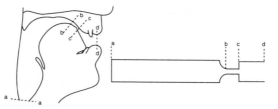

Fig. 8.10. The shape of the vocal tract in the vowel [i] as in *see* schematized as a Helmholtz resonator in which the body of the resonator is represented by the air contained in the pharynx (*a–b*), and the neck is formed by the channel between the tongue and the hard palate (*b–c*). In front of the Helmholtz resonator is a short tube, open at one end (*c–d*).

ously. This situation is shown schematically in figure 8.10. This is, of course, a considerable simplification of a complex shape.

It is possible to calculate the frequency of a Helmholtz resonance if one knows the volume of air in the body (*a–b* in the diagram), and the cross-sectional area and length of the neck (*b–c* in the diagram). If the area of the neck is A, the length is L, and the volume of the air in the body is V, then the formula for calculating the frequency is:

$$f = \frac{c}{2\pi} \sqrt{\left(\frac{A}{V L}\right)}. \qquad c = \text{the speed of sound.}$$

This formula can be used for calculating the resonances corresponding to some of the shapes of the vocal tract. The diagram in figure 8.10 might be taken to illustrate a constriction one cm long, in the area of the hard palate, 12–13 cm from the glottis. This would result in the volume of the cavity behind the constriction in the mouth and pharynx being about 60 cm^3. If the cross-sectional area of the constriction is 15 mm^2, then the frequency of the Helmholtz resonator would be a little over 280 Hz, an appropriate figure for the first formant of an [i] vowel. If the same size constriction is moved further back into the velar region, 10–12 cm from the glottis, the volume of the cavity would be reduced to about 50 cm³, and the frequency of the resonator would rise to 300 Hz, which is appropriate for an [u] vowel.

Another important case to study is what happens when we vary the size of the neck of the resonator, which in our case means when we vary the size of the channel between the tongue and the hard palate. Rather than the area of the neck of the resonator, A, we will consider the diameter, D, of the channel between the tongue and the roof of the mouth. If we assume that this channel is approximately circular, then the distance between the tongue and the roof of the mouth can be related to the area, A, by noting that the radius is half the diameter, so:

$$A = \pi \left(\frac{D}{2}\right)^2.$$

What we want to see is what happens when the tongue gets further away from the roof of the mouth, and the channel gets wider. Figure 8.11 shows the relation between the frequency produced and the distance of the tongue from the roof of the mouth, assuming the volume of air behind the tongue constriction remains the same. Of course, in a real speech movement, this volume would also change, but in order to understand the behavior of a Helmholtz resonator, it is easier to consider the effect of varying one thing at a time.

The solid point on the left of figure 8.11 is for a shape similar to that in the vowel [i]. For the sake of these calculations, the length of the constriction is taken to be 1.0 cm, and the volume of air behind the constriction is taken

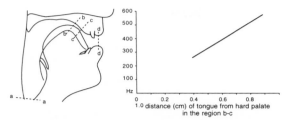

Fig. 8.11. The changes in the frequency of a Helmholtz resonator that occur when only the cross-sectional area of the neck is changed. The point on the left corresponds to a constriction appropriate for [i] (solid line). The point on the right is somewhat like that for [æ], but as only the tongue constriction is changed, the back cavity indicated by the dashed line is inappropriate.

to be 60 cm³. With these measurements and a narrow constriction the Helmholtz frequency is about 270 Hz. When the diameter of the channel is increased, as occurs when the tongue is lowered for more open vowels such as [ɪ] as in *bid*, or even lower vowels such as [ɛ] as in *bed*, the frequency increases. As we noted above, this diagram is not really suitable for demonstrating the formant frequencies that occur in these vowels, as the changes in the volume of air in the pharynx are not taken into account. Moreover, as the tongue moves further away from the hard palate, the shape of the vocal tract can no longer be considered to be that of a Helmholtz resonator, for which there has to be only a small body of air in the neck of the resonator. The diagram does, however, show how the low formant frequencies of high vowels can be accounted for, and the general way in which the first formant rises as these vowels become lower.

We will conclude this chapter by looking at the results of a more complex way of calculating the resonances of the vocal tract developed by the Swedish phonetician Gunnar Fant. Figure 8.12 is based on his (and later) calcu-

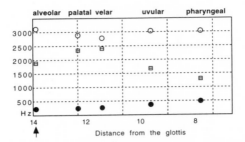

Fig. 8.12. The frequencies of the first three formants when there is a constriction in the vocal tract at different distances from the glottis. Frequencies of F1 are represented by solid points, those of the second formant by shaded points, and those of the third formant by open circles.

lations of the resonant frequencies—the formants—produced by a vocal tract modeled as a series of closely coupled tubes. We are therefore using a development of the model representing the vocal tract as coupled tubes in figure 8.7, and the model considering the vocal tract as (in part) a Helmholtz resonator as in figure 8.10.

The line of points above the arrow on the left of figure 8.12 represents the formants that are produced when the series of tubes simulates a constriction at a point almost 14 cm from the glottis, which is in the alveolar region. As you can see, the first formant is very low, the second formant is in the neighborhood of 1800 Hz, and the third formant is a little over 3,000 Hz. Whenever the articulators move toward a constriction of the vocal tract in the alveolar region, as they do when going from a vowel toward one of the consonants [t, d, n, l], the formant frequencies will move toward these values. If the constriction in the vocal tract is a little further back, in the palatal region, then the formant frequencies will be as indicated by the second column of points. As we saw earlier, these are very like the frequencies that occur in the production of the vowel [i] as in *see*. A constriction still further back, in the velar region, produces a situation in which the second and third formants are very close to each other. This is one of the marks of many velar consonants. In a word such as *gag*, the second and third formants seem to start from a common origin, move apart for the [æ] vowel, and then move together again for the final consonant. If the constriction is even further back, in the uvular region, then the second and third formants are not so close together, and there is a noticeable increase in the first formant. Finally, if the constriction is in the pharynx, as it is in the production of the vowel [ɑ] as in *father*, then the first two formants are beginning to have frequencies that are closer together.

All the frequencies shown in figure 8.12 were calculated on the assumption that the vocal tract had a very open lip position, corresponding to that in the vowel [ɑ] as in *father*. It is interesting to see what happens when we add lip rounding to each of these vocal tract shapes and recalculate the formant frequencies assuming a very close protruded lip position, with even more rounding than occurs in the vowel [u] as in *who*. The results are shown in figure 8.13. As may be seen, for a constriction in the very front part of the vocal tract, the major effect of lip rounding is to lower F3. In the palatal, velar, and uvular regions, there is a much greater effect on F2. A constriction in the velar region accompanied by lip rounding corresponds to the vocal tract shape for the vowel [u] as in *who*, or the semivowel [w]. The formants for this shape have frequencies of approximately 300, 800, and 2,600 Hz. Adding lip rounding has very little effect on the frequency of F1, wherever the constriction is; the small changes that do occur have not been shown in figure 8.13.

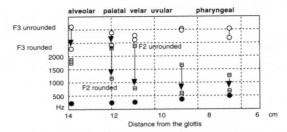

Fig. 8.13. The effect of adding lip rounding to each of the constrictions of the vocal tract for which the formant frequencies were shown in fig. 8.11. Changes in F1 are not noted, as they are very small.

Why does lip rounding have the largest effect on F3 sometimes, and on F2 at other times? The answer is that the lips are the boundary of the front cavity, the part of the vocal tract in front of the constriction produced by the tongue, so lip rounding primarily affects the resonance of this cavity. We can see this more clearly if we consider a slightly more elaborate version of figures 8.12 and 8.13, given in figure 8.14. This figure shows all the points in the previous figures, but this time they have been connected by lines, so that we can read off the formant frequencies produced by constrictions at intermediate distances from the glottis. If, for example, we want to know the frequencies of the first two formants when the lips are unrounded and there is a constriction 13 cm from the glottis (the upward-pointing arrow below the figure), then we could determine that they are at 250 Hz and 2,000 Hz, as indicated by the horizontal arrows on the left of the figure. Figure 8.14 also shows three intermediate degrees of lip rounding, indicated by the thinner lines between the heavy lines connecting the unrounded points and the shaded line connecting the rounded points, which we discussed previously.

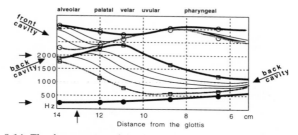

Fig. 8.14. The frequencies of the first three formants produced as a result of varying the location of a constriction in the vocal tract and also varying the degree of lip rounding. The most open position of the lips is represented by the heavy line, the most rounded position by the shaded line. The points marked by circles are those shown in fig. 8.12 and 8.13. The large arrow on the left points in the direction of frequencies associated with the front cavity; the arrow on the right points in the direction of frequencies associated with the back cavity. The smaller arrows mark the location of a particular constriction and the associated frequencies as discussed in the text.

Figure 8.14 makes the cavity resonances more apparent. At the top left of the diagram there is an arrow pointing diagonally downward, in the general direction of the frequencies that correspond to resonances of the front cavity. When this cavity is very short, as at the left of the figure when the tongue constriction is near the front of the mouth, the resonant frequency corresponds to the third formant. The second formant is the result of more complex modes of vibration associated with the constriction and the back cavity. As the constriction moves further back, the length of the front cavity increases and the third formant frequency decreases. At some point (depending on the lip rounding) there is a switch, and the second formant becomes associated with the front cavity, the third formant becoming a higher resonance of the remainder of the vocal tract. In regions where the third formant is associated with the front cavity, it is this formant that is primarily affected by lip rounding; otherwise it is the second formant.

For any given degree of lip rounding, there is a changeover region where the second and third formants change their cavity affiliations. In this region, moving the constriction a small amount backward or forward has comparatively little effect on the frequency of either the second or third formant. Vowels produced in regions where there can be comparatively large articulatory movements but only small formant changes have been termed quantal vowels. It has been suggested that such vowels are favored by languages because they have considerable acoustic stability despite articulatory variability. There are, however, problems with this notion. The tongue can be moved backward and forward without much effect on the formants in these vowels, but lowering the tongue slightly and thus varying the degree of constriction involved will cause major changes in the first formant frequency, as we saw in our discussion of Helmholtz resonators.

The resonances that can be associated with the back cavity are harder to see. When the constriction is at the front of the mouth, as on the left of figure 8.14, the second formant is the second resonance of the back cavity and increases as this cavity becomes smaller. When the constriction is in the back of the mouth, the first formant depends on the size of the back cavity. As the constriction moves back from the velar region through the uvular to the pharyngeal region, there is a noticeable effect of back cavity shortening, producing an increase in the frequency of the first formant.

Finally, we must always remember that the vocal tract has a very complex shape. In an introductory book such as this, it is convenient to think of it in terms of simple tubes and separable cavities. But descriptions made in this way are always gross simplifications. Anyone who looks at actual acoustic records of speech will rapidly find formant frequencies and other resonances that cannot be explained by these notions. What has been said here will do little more than help you start to understand the acoustics of speech production.

CHAPTER NINE
Digital Speech Processing

Nearly all speech processing involves computers, and anyone working in the field should understand how computers represent sound waves. Computers have to describe everything in terms of numbers. A sound wave must be reduced to a series of numbers representing the amplitude of the waveform at regular moments in time. Figure 9.1 shows how this is done. The wave in the upper part of the figure represents a sound wave as a continuously varying voltage that was recorded by a microphone during the production of the vowel [ɑ]. The lower part of the figure shows the magnitude of the voltage (the amplitude) when this wave is sampled at regular intervals, in this case 50 times in 1/100 of a second. The continuous wave can be represented in a computer by the set of discrete numbers (the samples) corresponding to these amplitudes. For example, sample number 1 is a large positive number, sample number 20 is a negative number, and sample number 50 is nearly zero. As there are 50 samples in 1/100 of a second, if the wave had lasted one second, there would have been 5,000 sample values to be stored.

The accuracy with which a sound wave can be stored in a computer is determined in part by the number of sam-

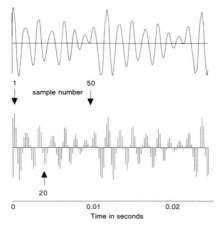

Fig. 9.1. Top: a continuously varying voltage recorded during the production of the vowel [ɑ}; below: lines corresponding to the size of this voltage (the amplitude) at regular intervals of time.

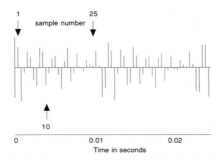

Fig. 9.2. The wave in the upper part of fig. 9.1 as represented by amplitude samples taken at a rate of 2,500 Hz.

ples taken per second. Figure 9.2 shows the samples that would represent the wave in figure 9.1 if there had been 2,500 samples in one second instead of 5,000, as in figure 9.1. In this case sample 25 occurs after 1/100 of a second.

A more accurate representation of this waveform is ob-

tained when it is sampled at a rate of 10,000 Hz, as shown
in figure 9.3, with sample 100 occurring after 1/100 of a
second. Note that the peaks in the wave are much more
well-defined.

If a wave is sampled at too slow a rate, then rapid variations that occur between samples cannot be represented.
In a high-frequency sound the amplitude variations will
be alternately positive and negative in a very short interval of time. To capture these rapid variations, the sampling rate must be very high. There must be at least one
positive and one negative sample before a frequency can
be said to be present in a sampled wave. Figure 9.4 shows
two repetitions of a 600 Hz damped wave, which is thus
much like the vowel [ɑ] as in *father*. The amplitude peaks
in this wave are 1/600 of a second apart. The upper part of
figure 9.4 shows what happens when this wave is sampled at a rate of 1,400 Hz (i.e., there are 1,400 samples per
second). A pair of samples is only 1/700 of a second apart,
so there is always at least one sample in each positive
peak in the wave, and one in each negative. The samples
may not represent the amplitudes in the damped wave

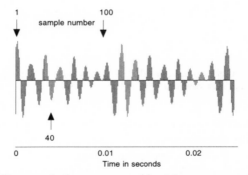

Fig. 9.3. The wave in the upper part of fig. 9.1 as represented by amplitude samples taken at a rate of 10,000 Hz.

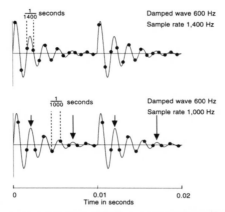

Fig. 9.4. A wave containing a 600 Hz component sampled at a rate of 1,400 Hz (upper part of the figure) and 1,000 Hz (lower part of the figure). The arrows mark peaks in the wave that are not represented when the sampling is at the lower rate.

very accurately, but at least they alternate positive and negative values at the same rate as the alternations in the damped wave. If the sample rate is dropped to 1,000 Hz, as in the lower part of figure 9.4, then pairs of samples are only 1/500 of a second apart, and it is no longer true that they alternate positive and negative values at the same rate as in the wave. The arrows in the bottom half of figure 9.4 mark a number of peaks that have not been sampled. If you tried to reconstitute the sampled wave by drawing a line joining the sample values, you would have a wave that did not have a 600 Hz frequency component. But if you draw a line joining the samples in the upper part of the figure you will produce a wave that has a different shape, but it at least has the right frequency.

The frequency which is half the sample rate is known as the Nyquist frequency. The Nyquist frequency must be at least equal to the highest frequency in the wave that

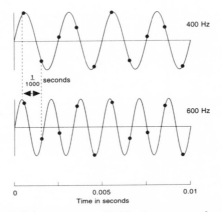

Fig. 9.5. Two different waves, a 400 Hz sine wave and a 600 Hz sine wave, both sampled at 1,000 Hz. The set of samples is exactly the same for both waves.

is being sampled. It is very important to ensure that a wave that is being sampled does not contain any frequencies above the Nyquist frequency. This point can be demonstrated by reference to figure 9.5, which shows the effect of sampling a 400 Hz sine wave and a 600 Hz sine wave at a sampling rate of 1,000 Hz. The 400 Hz wave is adequately sampled, with at least one positive and one negative sample for each peak. But the 600 Hz wave, which is above the 500 Hz Nyquist frequency, is not well represented. No sample occurs within some of the peaks. What is equally important and potentially disastrous if the samples are considered to be a true representation of the original wave is that the samples that do occur are exactly the same as those that represent the 400 Hz wave.

The incorrect representation of a frequency that is above the Nyquist frequency is known as aliasing. Whenever a sound is to be represented in digital terms on a computer, it is necessary to ensure that frequencies above the Nyquist frequency have been removed before sampling. If this is not done, samples from a wave that is a certain amount above the Nyquist frequency may be indistinguishable from those of another wave that is the same amount below the Nyquist frequency.

The highest frequencies that we are concerned with in speech are around 11,000 Hz. (Some of the components of sounds such as [s] may be higher, but they are not very significant, and they are not heard by many people over 40.) Consequently we can safely sample speech at 22,000 Hz—provided that we are sure that no higher frequencies are present from any source. We can remove higher frequencies by putting the signal through a filter that eliminates these components, a so-called low-pass filter. When we are interested only in vowels and other speech sounds that have little information above 5,000 Hz, we can sample at 10,000 Hz—again provided that the speech has been low-pass filtered to remove all higher frequencies. The standard sampling rate for high-fidelity music recordings is 44,000 Hz. This ensures that every sound which even the sharpest young ears can hear is present. Only small animals such as dogs and cats can hear frequencies above 22,000 Hz.

The sample rate is not the only factor that affects the fidelity of a sound stored on a computer. We also have to consider what numbers we choose to represent differences in amplitude. In sampling speech and putting it into a computer, we are doing the equivalent of putting a grid on a sound wave, as shown in figure 9.6, and storing the numbers corresponding to specific points on the grid. We are therefore quantizing the waveform in two dimensions, one corresponding to the time of each sample, and one corresponding to the amplitude at that time. The size of each amplitude step is obviously an important consid-

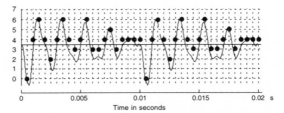

Fig. 9.6. A wave sampled at 5,000 Hz and with only 8 possible ampli-tude levels. The samples must be on the intersection of one of the grid lines showing the 8 possible amplitudes and one of the grid lines indi-cating one of the time intervals.

eration in the representation of the waveform. The smaller the size of each step, the more accurately the wave is represented. As well as sampling each wave suf-ficiently often, and thus making the time steps as small as necessary to record all the frequencies that are present, we also want to make sure that the size of each amplitude step is sufficiently small.

Because of the way in which they have to be stored in a computer, the sample amplitudes must be positive whole numbers (unsigned integers, if you wish to use the more technical term). In figure 9.6, for illustrative purposes, 8 possible levels of amplitude have been shown, reflecting the numbers 0–7. What is actually zero sound pressure would therefore correspond to midway between levels 3 and 4. This is a very inaccurate representation of the am-plitude, not capable of distinguishing many small varia-tions.

Figure 9.7 shows the same amplitude samples in the way that we have been diagramming them in previous figures, with the length of the line representing the am-plitude at that moment in time. In the upper part of figure 9.7 there are only 8 possible line lengths, corresponding

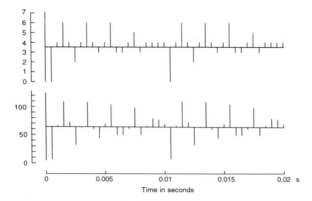

Fig. 9.7. Two different quantizations of the amplitude levels of the wave in fig. 9.6. In the upper part of the figure there are 8 possible amplitude levels as in fig. 9.6; in the lower part of the figure there are 128 possible amplitude levels.

to the 8 possible levels of amplitude in figure 9.6. The lower part of the figure shows the amplitude more accurately represented, with 128 possible amplitude levels.

In order to understand how differences in the number of possible amplitude levels affect computer analyses of sounds, we must consider how computers store numbers. Computers operate in terms of binary numbers called bits. The numbers 0 and 1 can be stored in one bit, but the numbers 2 and 3 require two bits, and 4, 5, 6, and 7 require three bits. Table 9.1 shows some numbers in the familiar decimal system and in binary terms. It may be seen that 0–7 require 3 bits, and 0–15 require 4 bits. Table 9.2 shows the number of bits required for storing larger numbers. As computers typically regard 8 bits as one computer word (one byte), it is important to note that 256 possible amplitude levels (0–255) require 8 bits, and 65,536 levels (0–65,535) require 16 bits (two words).

Table 9.1 Decimal and Binary Numbers

Decimal	Binary	Number of Bits
0	0	1
1	1	1
2	10	2
3	11	2
4	100	3
5	101	3
6	110	3
7	111	3
8	1000	4
9	1001	4
10	1010	4
11	1011	4
12	1100	4
13	1101	4
14	1110	4
15	1111	4

Table 9.2 The Number of Bits Required for a Given Range of Numbers

Range of Numbers	Number of Bits
1–32	5
1–64	6
1–128	7
1–256	8
1–512	9
1–1,024	10
1–2,048	11
1–4,096	12
1–8,192	13
1–16,384	14
1–32,768	15
1–65,536	16

Most computer sampling is in terms of whole words, typically with 8-bit quantization (256 possible levels), or 16-bit quantization (65,536 possible levels). We can use these numbers to calculate the difference in dB between the smallest sound and the largest sound that a computer can store in different circumstances. With 8-bit sampling, the ratio between the largest sound and the smallest sound will be 255 to 1. In chapter 4 we saw that the difference in dB between two sounds is 20 times the log of their voltage ratio. So if the largest amplitude is 255 and the smallest is 1, this ratio is 255. The log of 255 is 2.4, so the difference in dB is $20 \times 2.4 = 48$ dB. With 16-bit sampling the ratio between the largest sound and the smallest sound will be 65,535 to 1. The log of 65,535 is 4.8, so the difference in dB is $20 \times 4.8 = 96$ dB. The standard quantization for high-fidelity audio digitization is 16 bits, allowing a range of 96 dB, almost the full range of intensities that the human ear can hear without pain.

If we sample speech at 22,000 Hz, using 16-bit sampling, we will need $22,000 \times 2 = 44,000$ bytes (i.e., 44 K computer words) for each second. A minute of speech will need $44,000 \times 60 = 2,840$ K on the computer—almost 3 meg, in computer terminology. Assuming a reading speed of 140 words a minute, and an average of 5.3 characters (counting spaces and punctuation) for these 140 words, as is typical in this book, the same text when written will be 740 characters. Each character can be stored in a single byte, so the written text will require 740 bytes, or less than 1 K of memory on the computer. Reducing high-quality speech to writing loses all the nuances of information conveyed by spoken language, but it also involves almost a three thousand to one reduction in computer storage.

Windows

We will conclude this chapter with two examples of basic computer speech processing techniques. The first is a notion that is called windowing. When we analyze a spoken sentence, we often want to consider a section of the sound associated with a particular segment. If we want to know the formants of a vowel, for example, we want to make a Fourier analysis of just a few cycles that are typical of the middle of the vowel. We do this by putting a window—a mask with a hole in it—over the wave. The shape of the window is important. If it is rectangular, we might cut out a piece of the wave, as shown in figure 9.8. Many implementations of a Fourier analysis assume that the parts of the wave outside the window are zero. They would treat the wave shown in the lower part of figure 9.8 as if it had an abrupt beginning and ending. As we saw earlier, waves with abrupt changes have considerable high-frequency components. An analysis of the part of the wave within a rectangular window would include these higher frequencies and would thus be in error, as they are not present in the original wave. We can deal

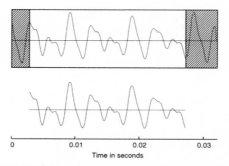

Fig. 9.8. A rectangular window superimposed on a wave (upper part) so that only the lower part is available for analysis.

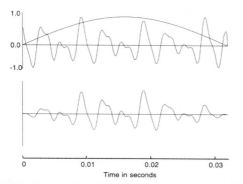

Fig. 9.9. A Hanning window superimposed on a wave (upper part), and the result of multiplying that wave by the window (lower part).

with this problem by using a more sophisticated form of windowing, as discussed below.

Figure 9.9 illustrates another way of representing a window. Instead of showing the piece of the wave that is being viewed, we have superimposed a curve that goes from 0.0 up to 1.0 and then down to 0.0 again. If each point on the wave is multiplied by the value of the corresponding point in the superimposed curve, then the wave shown in the lower part of figure 9.9 will be produced. At the beginning and end of the window, the original wave is multiplied by zero or a very small number, so the windowed wave is zero or very small. In the middle of the window, the original wave is multiplied by 1.0 and is therefore unaffected. In a broad area around the center of the window, the wave is changed very little.

The particular curve used for the window shape in figure 9.9 is called a Hanning function. Similar functions often named in the speech analysis literature are the Hamming and Blackman windows. Each of these is simply a way of smoothing the edges of the piece of the waveform being analyzed. Almost any way of specifying a curve that rises smoothly from near zero and reaches a plateau around 1.0 before descending smoothly to near zero again is satisfactory for most forms of analysis. It is easy to apply a window to a digitized waveform in which each point is represented by a number. It is a simple multiplication which can be done on a computer.

Autocorrelation

The last computer process that we will discuss in this chapter is known as autocorrelation. It can be used in finding the fundamental frequency of a waveform. Consider a speech wave such as that shown at the top of figure 9.10 (the same wave as in figure 9.9). This is a real speech wave, and hence it does not repeat itself exactly every 1/100 of a second when a new glottal pulse occurs. Nevertheless, it is possible to see that this is a speech wave with a fundamental frequency of about 100 Hz and a formant frequency of about 300–400 Hz corresponding

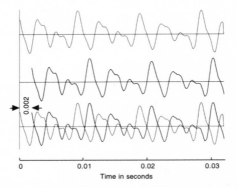

Fig. 9.10. A speech wave (top), a copy of the same wave delayed by 0.002 seconds (middle), and these two waves superimposed on each other (bottom).

to the smaller peaks in the damped wave produced by the glottal pulse. Now consider the same wave delayed by an arbitrary amount (0.0035 s), as in the middle of figure 9.10. There is not much in common between these two waves, as can be seen in the bottom of the figure, where they are shown superimposed on one another.

A very different situation occurs when the waves are compared with one another after a delay corresponding to the interval between glottal pulses, as shown in figure 9.11. The correlation between these two waves is not perfect, for a number of reasons: the interval between pulses is not constant; there was probably some articulatory movement producing changes in the formants; and there will be an interaction between the decaying wave from one pulse and the onset of the damped wave due to the next pulse. Nevertheless, there is good agreement in the parts of the wave corresponding to one pulse and the next.

We can see from figures 9.10 and 9.11 that when we de-

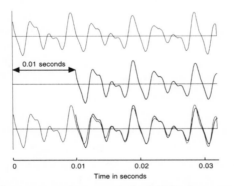

Fig. 9.11. The same speech wave as in fig. 9.10 (top), a copy of this wave delayed by 0.01 seconds (middle), and these two waves superimposed on each other (bottom).

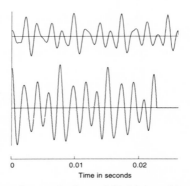

Fig. 9.12. The speech wave in figure 9.10 (top), and its autocorrelation function (bottom).

lay a wave by different amounts and compare it with itself, the degree of agreement varies in accordance with the delay. The autocorrelation function is a measure of the degree of agreement for a number of different delays. Figure 9.12 is a plot of this function for the wave shown in figures 9.11 and 9.12, when the delay is varied from a single point to an amount corresponding to about one-third of the whole window. When the delay is only one point, as at the left of the figure, there is good agreement between the delayed and the original wave, which is not surprising because adjacent points in the wave do not differ very much. The next major peak comes when the delay is 0.01 seconds. There is another major peak when it is 0.02 seconds, and yet another when it is 0.03 seconds. In between these peaks there are smaller peaks that arise from delays corresponding to the formant frequencies.

The autocorrelation function provides a very good way of determining the pitch of a sound. The first major peak occurs at a time (0.01 seconds in the present example) which is the reciprocal of the fundamental frequency (100

Hz in this example). There are occasional problems in using this method of pitch extraction in that, for example, the peaks due to correlations associated with the formants may occasionally be fairly large. But it is usually much easier to find major peaks in the autocorrelation function than it is to find them in the original waveform. It is even easier to find the peaks in the autocorrelation function if we can apply it to a waveform from which much of the variation due to the formants has been removed. We will discuss a way in which this can be done in the final chapter.

CHAPTER TEN
Fourier Analysis

Most of this book has avoided a mathematical approach to acoustic problems, relying instead on graphical techniques wherever possible. In these last two chapters we will continue to presume that readers have never known, or have forgotten, all but the most basic mathematical concepts. We will, however, present enough mathematics to demonstrate how computers are used to analyze speech. We will do this without using calculus or matrix algebra. But for those who are interested, we will present fragments of computer programs that embody the ideas involved. The computer programs can be safely skipped, but they should be understandable even by those who have never looked at a computer program before. It is useful for anyone working in acoustic phonetics to learn something about programming.

Sine Waves

So far we have not defined a sine wave. We have simply drawn diagrams of sine waves showing that they are functions with a particular shape, smoothly increasing and decreasing. Before we can go much further in understanding the analysis of speech, we must describe this shape more explicitly, in simple mathematical terms. We will begin by considering the motion of a point, P, moving around the circumference of a circle of radius a at a uniform rate of one cycle in 1/100 of a second, as shown in figure 10.1. This point will be making 100 revolutions per second, and, as we will see, it can be regarded as specifying a sine wave of 100 Hz.

If we draw a right triangle with its base on the horizontal diameter of the circle (the x axis) and its apex at the point P, we can define the length y as the distance from the point P to this diameter. As P goes round the circle, this distance will vary. When P is near (1) on the circle, y will be very small; and when P is near (2), it will approach its maximum, which is a, the radius of the circle. If we consider distances below to be represented by negative numbers, then y will vary between a maximum of $+a$ and a minimum of $-a$, at a rate of 100 times per second. We should also note that when the point P is near (1) on the circle, the length y will be small but varying rapidly, and when P is near (2), y will be large but varying more slowly as it approaches and moves away from its maximum. The variation in the value of y is what mathematicians define

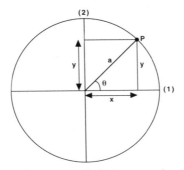

Fig. 10.1. A point moving counterclockwise around a circle at a rate of 100 cycles per second.

as a *sine function*. This function depends on the angle θ, which is increasing at a constant rate as the point *P* moves around the circle. In mathematical terms, the ratio between *y* and the radius of the circle is defined as the sine of the angle θ. The sine of a particular angle is written as sin θ, so $y/a = \sin θ$, and $y = a \sin θ$. The angle θ increases uniformly with time; twice around the circle is equivalent to 720°, and three times around it is 1,080°, so a graph of *y* as a function of time is a graph of a sine wave as shown in figure 10.2.

The (maximum) amplitude of the wave in figure 10.2 is *a*. As the point *P* is making 100 revolutions per second, we can also note the variations in sin θ as a function of time. When θ is 90°, *y* will be the same as *a*, and sin $θ = a/a$, which is 1. When θ is 180° *y* is zero, and sin $θ = 0/a = 0$. When θ is 270°, *y* is −*a*, and sin $θ = -a/a = -1$. The angle θ will go from 0° to 360° during one cycle, as shown in figure 10.2, and continue increasing as long as the wave lasts.

Now let us think how a sine wave might be represented in a computer. As we saw in the last chapter, it will be stored as the amplitudes of a number of discrete points. How many points there are in a complete cycle of

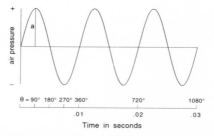

Fig. 10.2. A sine wave with amplitude *a* and frequency 100 Hz.

a sine wave depends on both the sample rate and the frequency of the sine wave. If the sample rate is 10,000 Hz (i.e., there are 10,000 samples in one second), and the frequency is 100 Hz (i.e., there are 100 cycles in one second), then each cycle will have 10,000/100 = 100 points. More generally, the number of points in a cycle, N, is sample rate/frequency (Hz).

We saw earlier that the amplitude, y, at each point in a sine wave depends on $a \sin \theta$, where a is the maximum amplitude, and the angle θ varies between 0° and 360° in a cycle. Now consider any point n, which is one of the N points that has been sampled within the cycle. We can represent the relation between the point n and the angle θ as shown in figure 10.3.

Thus $n/N = \theta/360$, and $\theta = (n * 360)/N$.

We can now see that the amplitude, y_n, of this point $= a \sin (n * 360/N)$.

At this point we should deal with a slight complication if we want to see how a computer might store points corresponding to those in a sine wave. When making calculations concerning waves, it is more usual to represent angles in terms of radians rather than degrees. A radian, like a degree, is a measure of an angle. A radian is formally defined as the ratio between the length of an arc and the radius of a circle. If the radius is r, the circumference is $2\pi r$, so this "arc" (i.e., the circumference) defines an angle of $2\pi r/r = 2\pi$ radians. If a complete circle

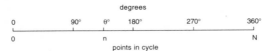

Fig. 10.3. The relation between an angle θ in a complete cycle of 360° and a sample point n in a wave that has N sample points in one cycle.

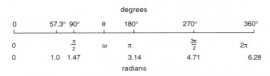

Fig. 10.4. The relation between angles in degrees and in radians.

(360°) is 2π radians, then 180° is π radians, or approximately 3.14 radians, and a right angle (90°) is $\pi/2$ radians, which is 1.57 radians. Putting all this in the form of a diagram as in figure 10.4, we can see that one radian = 57.3°.

If a point is moving around a circle with a frequency of 100 Hz, it will pass through 100 times 2π radians in a second. In other words, it will have a frequency of 200π radians. Put more generally, a frequency of f Hz corresponds to an angular velocity of $2\pi f$ radians per second. In technical papers on the acoustics of speech, the frequencies are usually expressed in terms of what is known as the angular frequency, in radians per second, often represented by the Greek character omega, ω. Similarly, when making calculations in a computer we need the frequency to be expressed in radians. When considering the amplitude of the point n, which is one of the N points that has been sampled within a cycle, we can represent the relationship as shown in figure 10.5.

Thus $n/N = \omega/2\pi$ and $\omega = (n * 2\pi)/N$.

Accordingly we can rewrite our expression for the amplitude, y_n, and say:

$$y_n = a \sin((n * 2\pi)/N).$$

We can summarize all this, and learn a little about computer programming, by using these expressions to

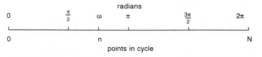

Fig. 10.5. The relation between an angle ω in a complete cycle of 2π radians and a sample point n in a wave that has N sample points in one cycle.

write a program that draws a graph of a sine wave. If you wish, you can skip the remainder of this section and go straight on to the section headed "Cosine waves." However, if you want to be sure that you can really understand something, you should learn to write a computer program to do it. In that way you will be sure that there are no hidden assumptions that you have missed.

Here is a version of a program in the computer language Pascal. It will draw a line on the computer screen corresponding to a 100 Hz sine wave, starting from an arbitrary point on the screen designated as (x,y), which on my computer is convenient to make as 10 points from the left ($x = 10$), and 150 points down from the top ($y = 150$). By referring to what has been said above about the relation between the number of points in a cycle, the sample rate, and the frequency, you should be able to follow each statement, even if you have done no computer programming before.

This program is not the most efficient way of plotting the graph; a few extra steps have been put in to make it more readable.

```
program SineWave;
const {The terms that we will consider to be constants, fixed for
      this program}
x = 10;
y = 150;
SampleRate = 10000;
```

```
Frequency = 100;
Amplitude = 127;          {This is an arbitrary amplitude
                          factor—under half 256, which is conve-
                          nient for computers that use a maxi-
                          mum of 256 values}
pi = 3.14;                {an approximation for π}
var                       {The types of variables that we will
                          need}
pointsInCycle, pointAmp, n : integer; {all these are whole numbers}
realAmp, angle : real;   {a real number is stored as a number
                          with a decimal point included.
                          Only integers can be used in computer
                          graphs}
begin
pointsInCycle := round (SampleRate/Frequency); {rounded off
                                            to an integer}
moveTo (x,y);             {move to the starting point of the graph}
for n := 1 to pointsInCycle do
        {we want to loop through the following for each point}
    begin
        angle := (2 * pi * n/pointsInCycle;  {the angle in radians
                                        is the 2 π times the
                                        proportion of the
                                        way through the cy-
                                        cle.}
                                        { n = 1 the first time
                                        through the loop,
                                        n = 2 the second
                                        time through, and
                                        so on, increasing
                                        till n = pointsInCy-
                                        cle.}
        realAmp := Amplitude * sin ( angle );{the real amplitude
                                        for this (and each)
                                        point}
        pointAmp := round ( real Amp );  {turn the amplitude
                                        into an integer}
        lineTo (x + n, y − pointAmp);    {draw a line to this
                                        point}
    end;
end.
```

If speed were a consideration in the running of this program, we could reduce the number of multiplications and divisions by combining some of these statements and by defining an additional variable just once, near the beginning of the program:

radianFactor = 2 * pi/pointsInCycle

Then in the loop that applies to every point we could say:

pointAmp := round (Amplitude * sin (radianFactor * n));

Cosine Waves

When we come to analyze speech sounds, we need to consider cosine waves as well as sine waves. The cosine of an angle is the ratio of the side adjacent to the angle (in a right triangle) and the hypotenuse. Referring back to figure 10.1, we can note that:

$$y = a \sin \theta.$$
$$x = a \cos \theta.$$

When θ is zero, x is the radius of the circle, a, and when θ is 90°, then x is zero. Figure 10.6 shows a sine wave and a cosine wave, both dependent on the same angle θ. Note that they have the same shape, but the cosine wave lags

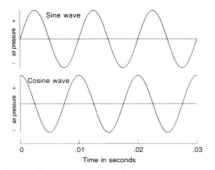

Fig. 10.6. A sine and a cosine wave with the same frequency (100 Hz).

behind the sine wave by a quarter of a cycle, i.e., an interval corresponding to $\theta = 90°$. Both sine and cosine waves are called sinusoidal waves; they have what is called a difference in phase.

As we saw in earlier chapters, variations in air pressure corresponding to different waves can be added together. A sine wave and a cosine wave added together produce another sinusoidal wave, with a larger amplitude and with a phase that is intermediate between that of the sine wave and the cosine wave, as shown in figure 10.7.

If the cosine wave is smaller than the sine wave, the phase of the resulting wave will be more like that of the sine wave, i.e., closer to 0 than to 90°, as shown in figure 10.8.

But if the cosine wave is larger than the sine wave, the resulting sinusoidal wave will have a phase closer to that of the cosine wave, i.e., nearer to 90°, as in figure 10.9.

Fourier Analysis

As we saw in chapter 4, complex waves can be described as the sum of a number of sinusoidal compo-

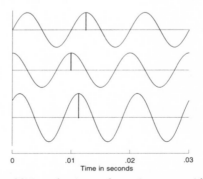

Fig. 10.7. The addition of a sine and a cosine wave with the same frequency.

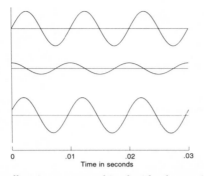

Fig. 10.8. A small cosine wave combined with a larger sine wave, both having a frequency of 100 Hz.

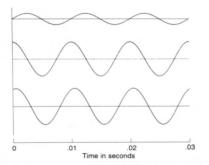

Fig. 10.9. A small sine wave combined with a larger cosine wave, both having a frequency of 100 Hz.

nents. (In that chapter we did not consider cosine waves and referred to all components as sine waves; now that we see how waves can differ in phase, we will consider both sine and cosine waves as possible components.) Consider the complex wave in figure 10.10. How do we determine its component frequencies?

Our first step in solving this problem is to delimit the section of the wave we will analyze by applying a win-

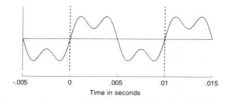

Fig. 10.10. A complex wave which is considered to be a single period that was repeated indefinitely in the past, and will be repeated indefinitely in the future.

dow, as discussed in the previous chapter. For simplicity, we will use a rectangular window, so that we consider only the part of the wave between the dashed lines. But also for simplicity, we have carefully chosen this window so that it encloses a single period. We will assume that this period was repeated indefinitely in the past and will be repeated indefinitely in the future. The procedure that we will use is what is known as a Discrete Fourier Transform (DFT).

As the window has a duration of 1/100 of a second, we can see that the repeated waveform has a fundamental frequency of 100 Hz. The first step in the analysis is to see how well this wave correlates with a 100 Hz sine wave with a standard amplitude, such as the one shown superimposed in figure 10.11.

The correlation between two waves is a measure of how well the two waves are similar at every point in a single cycle. The correlation is calculated by first multiplying each point on the one wave by the corresponding point on the other and then summing the results of all these multiplications. (The mathematical term for this number is the dot product.)

Consider how this would work if we wanted to calculate the correlation between two sine waves with differ-

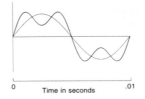

Fig. 10.11. A 100 Hz sine wave superimposed on the wave in fig. 10.10.

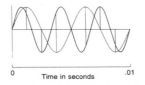

Fig. 10.12. Two sine waves, one with a frequency of 200 Hz (light line), and the other with a frequency of 300 Hz (heavy line).

ent frequencies, as in figure 10.12. We want to consider the amplitude at every point on the two waves, but for illustrative purposes we will consider the amplitudes only at the times indicated by the vertical lines in figure 10.12. These amplitudes are as shown in table 10.1, using an arbitrary scale.

Given the amplitudes and times in the first three columns, we now have to calculate the products of the two amplitudes, which are as shown in the fourth column of the table. Then, in each row, the final column shows the sum of this product and the previous products. The correlation is based on the sum of the products for every point on the two waves. Because there are as many positive products as there are negative, this sum is zero when totaled over a single cycle of the sine wave with the lower

Table 10.1 The Amplitudes, Their Products, and the Accumulating
Sum of These Products for a Number of Points in the Waves in Fig. 10.12

Time(s)	200 Hz Amplitude	300 Hz Amplitude	Product	Accumulating Sum of Products
0.00125	80	57	4560	4560
0.00250	0	−80	0	4560
0.00375	−80	57	−4560	0
0.00500	0	0	0	0
0.00625	80	−57	−4560	−4560
0.00750	0	80	0	−4560
0.00875	−80	−57	4560	0
0.01000	0	0	0	0

frequency. (Obviously it is still zero when totaled over two cycles, as in this figure.)

The correlation between any two sine waves of different frequencies will always be zero. Every positive product is matched by an equal negative product, as further illustrated in figure 10.13. In the top part of figure 10.13 there are two sine waves, one with a frequency of 100 Hz (light line), and the other with a frequency of 500 Hz (heavy line). An (arbitrary) amplitude scale has been added to take the place of the table showing the amplitudes in the previous discussion. The lower part of the figure indicates graphically the result of multiplying every point on one wave by the corresponding point on the other. Thus at time *a* both amplitudes are 100 on this arbitrary scale, so their product is 10,000. At time *b* the 100 Hz wave has a slightly smaller amplitude, but the 500 Hz wave has a large negative amplitude, so the product is a large negative number. At time *c* both waves have comparatively small negative amplitudes, so the product is positive. At any time when either of the waves has a zero

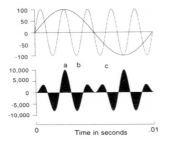

Fig. 10.13. Upper part: two sine waves, one with a frequency of 500 Hz (light line), and the other with a frequency of 100 Hz (heavy line). Lower part: the cross product of these two waves.

amplitude, the product is also zero. When all these products are added together (i.e., the dark shaded areas in the lower figure are added together), the result is zero. In mathematical terms, this zero correlation is what is meant by saying that sine waves of different frequencies are orthogonal. They can always be considered as adding an independent contribution to a complex wave.

This is the basis of Fourier analysis. As sine waves are orthogonal, the *only* correlation between a sine wave and a complex wave will be with the components of the complex wave that have the same frequency as the sine wave. With this in mind, we can now return to the analysis of the complex wave shown in figure 10.10. We will first work out the correlation between this wave and the 100 Hz wave, considering only selected points, as shown in figure 10.14, so that we can produce a table similar to table 10.1. The values we require are shown in table 10.2.

This time all the cross products are zero or positive, and their sum is far from zero. As is obvious from both figure 10.14 and table 10.2, the 100 Hz sine wave and the

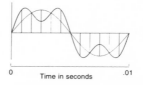

0   .01
                    Time in seconds

Fig. 10.14. A complex wave with a fundamental frequency of 100 Hz and a sine wave with the same frequency, showing a number of points which will be used in the calculation of the correlation.

Table 10.2 The Amplitudes, Their Products, and the Accumulating Sum of These Products for a Number of Points in the Waves in Fig. 10.14

Time(s)	Complex Amplitude	100 Hz Amplitude	Product	Accumulating Sum of Products
0.00083	60	30	1800	1800
0.00167	52	52	2704	4504
0.00250	30	60	1800	6304
0.00333	52	52	2704	9008
0.00417	60	30	1800	10808
0.00500	0	0	0	10808
0.00583	−60	−30	1800	12608
0.00667	−52	−52	2704	15312
0.00750	−30	−60	1800	17112
0.00833	−52	−52	2704	19816
0.00917	−60	−30	1800	21616
0.01000	0	0	0	21616

complex wave are highly correlated. If we had drawn a diagram like that in figure 10.13, all the dark areas would have been above the zero line.

Our next task is to see how well the complex wave is correlated with other harmonics of the 100 Hz fundamental. Figure 10.15 and table 10.3 show the answer. It is apparent that if we multiply every point on the complex wave by every point on the 200 Hz sine wave, there will

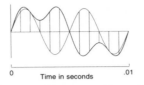

Fig. 10.15. A complex wave with a fundamental frequency of 100 Hz and a sine wave with a frequency of 200 Hz, showing a number of points which will be used in the calculation of the correlation.

Table 10.3 The Amplitudes, Their Products, and the Accumulating Sum of These Products for a Number of Points in the Waves in Fig. 10.15

Time(s)	Complex Amplitude	200 Hz Amplitude	Product	Accumulating Sum of Products
0.00083	60	52	3120	3120
0.00167	52	52	2704	5824
0.00250	30	0	0	5824
0.00333	52	−52	−2704	3120
0.00417	60	−52	−3120	0
0.00500	0	0	0	0
0.00583	−60	52	−3120	−3120
0.00667	−52	52	−2704	−5824
0.00750	−30	0	0	−5824
0.00833	−52	−52	2704	−3120
0.00917	−60	−52	3120	0
0.01000	0	0	0	0

be no correlation. Every positive point is matched by an equal negative point.

When we compare the complex wave with a 300 Hz wave, the situation is as shown in figure 10.16 and table 10.4. There are some negative but even more larger positive products. Overall, the correlation is positive, but it is not as great as with the 100 Hz wave. The total of the cross products is half that of the total for the 100 Hz wave

0   Time in seconds   .01

Fig. 10.16. A complex wave with a fundamental frequency of 100 Hz and a sine wave with a frequency of 300 Hz, showing a number of points which will be used in the calculation of the correlation.

Table 10.4 The Amplitudes, Their Products, and the Accumulating Sum of These Products for a Number of Points in the Waves in Fig. 10.16

Time(s)	Complex Amplitude	300 Hz Amplitude	Product	Accumulating Sum of Products
0.00083	60	60	3600	3600
0.00167	52	0	0	3600
0.00250	30	−60	−1800	1800
0.00333	52	0	0	1800
0.00417	60	60	3600	5400
0.0050	0	0	0	5400
0.0058	−60	−60	3600	9000
0.00667	−52	0	0	9000
0.0075	−30	60	−1800	7200
0.00833	−52	0	0	7200
0.00917	−60	−60	3600	10800
0.01000	0	0	0	10800

(which is correct, as this complex wave was synthesized by adding a 100 Hz sine wave and a 300 Hz sine wave with half the amplitude).

Again, so that we can see exactly how the cross product is generated, we will consider how this can be done by a computer program (and again, if you wish, you can skip the next couple of paragraphs). In this example of a fragment of a program we will take it that the values representing the complex wave are stored in an array in a variable we will call complexWave, with the nth value being stored in complexWave[n]. These values might be the result of analog to digital (A/D) conversion. The corresponding set of values for the sine wave will be stored in an array sineWave, with the nth value being stored in sineWave[n]. We have already seen how we can calculate the values for a sine wave. When we need them to be stored in an array with members such as sineWave[n], we can use a section of code such as:

```
radianFactor := 2.0 * Pi/pointsInCycle;
    for n := 1 to pointsInCycle do
      sineWave[n] := sin(n * radianFactor) * Amplitude;
```

Now all we need is a section of code that will take each of the points in the complex wave, multiply the amplitude of that point by the value of the corresponding point in the sine wave, and add the result of the multiplication to the result of the previous multiplication, just as we did in table 10.4. Assuming that all the variables have been declared elsewhere, we can say:

```
accumulatingAmplitude := 0; { begin by setting the amplitude
                              to zero }
for n := 1 to pointsInCycle do {now look at every point, and add
                                its effect}
    accumulatingAmplitude := complex Wave[n] * sineWave[n]
                             + accumulatingAmplitude;
```

So far we have been considering a very simple example, in which we happened to have exactly one period to analyze, and the complex wave happened to have the same phase as the 100 Hz sine wave. But the complex wave might have started at a different time, as shown in the upper part of figure 10.17. In this case the complex wave has exactly the same shape as the complex wave in figure 10.10, which we have been analyzing in subsequent fig-

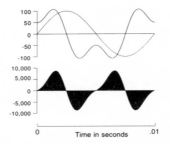

Fig. 10.17. Upper part: a complex wave that has the same shape as the wave in fig. 10.10 but has a different phase in relation to a superimposed 100 Hz sine wave. Lower part: a graphical representation of the result of multiplying each point on the complex wave by the corresponding point on the 100 Hz sine wave.

ures, but it has a different phase relative to the 100 Hz sine wave. As a result, there is no correlation between the two waves, as you can see from the lower part of figure 10.17, which is a graphical representation of the results of multiplying each point on the complex wave by the corresponding point on the 100 Hz wave. For every positive result of this multiplication, there is a corresponding negative point. When we sum the products over a complete cycle the result is zero.

This does not mean, however, that the complex wave has no 100 Hz component. It has zero correlation with a sine wave of the same frequency, but it has a high correlation with a 100 Hz cosine wave, as can instantly be seen from figure 10.18. In this case all the cross products are positive.

In general, as we do not know the relative phases of the complex wave and the components, we will have to consider the correlation with both the sine wave and the corresponding cosine wave. If we want to know the amplitude of a component in a complex wave, we must in some

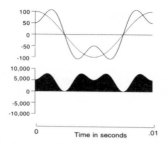

Fig. 10.18. Upper part: the complex wave in fig. 10.17 and a superimposed 100 Hz cosine wave. Lower part: a graphical representation of the result of multiplying each point on the complex wave by the corresponding point on the 100 Hz cosine wave.

way sum the amplitudes of the sine and cosine components. Referring back to our definition of sine and cosine waves in terms of a point moving around a circle, we can see how to do this. If, as shown in figure 10.19, the amplitude of a point on a sine wave is x, and that of a point on a cosine wave is y, then the amplitude of the point on the sinusoidal wave is a, where (by Pythagoras) $a = \sqrt{(x^2 + y^2)}$, or $(x^2 + y^2)^{1/2}$.

We usually want to express the relative amplitudes of the components of a complex wave in dB with reference to some arbitrary amplitude. Let us suppose that this arbitrary amplitude has a value of one unit. We saw earlier (in chap. 6) that the dB difference between two sounds was 20 times the common log of the amplitude ratio between the two sounds. If the reference sound has an amplitude of one, this would be $20 \log_{10} a$. As $a = (x^2 + y^2)^{1/2}$ the amplitude in dB relative to one unit is $20 \log_{10}((x^2 + y^2)^{1/2})$, which can be simplified to $10 \log_{10} (x^2 + y^2)$.

This amplitude will be an arbitrary number. We can say that it is the amplitude in dB in the sense that the ampli-

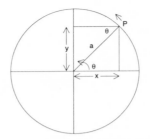

Fig. 10.19. The relation between the amplitude, y, of a point on a sine wave, the corresponding point, x, on a cosine wave of the same frequency, and the point, a, on the sinusoidal wave that is the result of summing the sine and cosine components. $a = \sqrt{(x^2 + y^2)} = (x^2 + y^2)^{1/2}$.

tude of other components calculated in the same way will be in dB with respect to the same arbitrary base. So we will be able to assess the *relative* amplitudes (in dB) of the various components of the complex wave. Usually the component with the highest amplitude is taken to be zero, and other components are expressed in dB down from that. We will now extend our fragment of a computer program that gives the amplitude of the sinusoidal components and say:

```
sineAmplitude := 0; { in this version there are two intermediate }
cosAmplitude := 0; { variables used for accumulating sums }
radianFactor := 2.0 * Pi/pointsInCycle;
for n := 1 to pointsInCycle do {for each point, calculate and sum
     cross products}
     begin
         sineAmplitude := complexWave[n] *
                         sin( n * radianFactor ) + sineAmplitude;
         cosAmplitude := complexWave[n] *
                         cos( n * radianFactor ) + cosAmplitude;
     end;
{Now get the sum of the squares of these, and calculate 10 times
the log of this number}
```

ComponentAmplitude: = 10*$\log_{10}$(sineAmplitude*
    sineAmplitude + cosAmplitude*cosAmplitude);

So far we have been analyzing a fairly simple wave, one with virtually only two components. (There are, in theory, an infinite number of components, but in the complex wave we have been analyzing only two of them have any amplitude.) Moreover, in the interval being analyzed, there was exactly one period of the one component and there were exactly three periods of the other component. But in general, when we are analyzing speech, the situation is not so simple.

In the type of analysis we are considering, the Discrete Fourier Transform, we look for components in the complex wave that are multiples of the fundamental frequency determined by the window length. In the previous example the window length was 1/100 of a second, so we looked for components that were multiples of 100 Hz. This was appropriate, as the components were in fact 100 Hz and 300 Hz. But when we do not know anything about the signal to be analyzed, there is no reason to expect a convenient relationship such as this. There may not be such a good match between the analysis components, which are defined as multiples of the frequency determined by the window length and the harmonic structure of the signal, which will be determined by whatever the fundamental frequency of the wave happens to be.

Consider the analysis of the speech wave shown in figure 10.20. We do not know the fundamental frequency of this wave and simply have to take an arbitrary piece and analyze that. This window length will determine the frequency of all the components in the analysis, in that they must all be harmonics of the corresponding fundamental.

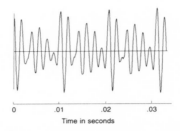

Fig. 10.20. A complex wave that is to be analyzed.

We will take it that we have a digital representation of the waveform sampled at 10,000 Hz. As we saw in the previous chapter, if the sample rate is 10,000 Hz, the highest frequency that can be present is half that, i.e., 5,000 Hz. We will consider an arbitrary window of 256 points of this wave, as shown in figure 10.21. At that sample rate, 256 points corresponds to a window length of 25.6 ms. If a single period is 25.6 ms, then the frequency (the number of periods in a second) is 1,000/25.6 = 39 Hz. Putting this another way, we can say that the frequency is Sample rate/window length, which in our case is 10,000/256 = 39 Hz.

In a Discrete Fourier Transform (DFT), the first component in the analysis is the sine wave that will just fit into the window. We should emphasize here that this is a component in the analysis, and it is not the same as what we took to be a component in previous chapters. Earlier we were considering the wave as a whole, and not just the small piece in a window. When we were considering longer stretches, we could say that the components were harmonics of the fundamental frequency defined by the rate of vibration of the vocal cords. In doing this we had to pretend that each period was an exact repetition of the surrounding periods; we were in fact pretending that

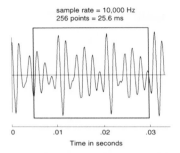

sample rate = 10,000 Hz
256 points = 25.6 ms

Fig. 10.21. A complex wave with a superimposed window.

each period was something that could be treated as if it had been repeated throughout all past and all future time. When we are making a Discrete Fourier Transform, we are in a similar situation. We take the sinusoidal wave (with both sine and cosine components) that will just fit into the window as the fundamental frequency for the analysis. In the case we are considering, it is a wave with a frequency of 39 Hz, as shown in figure 10.22.

The second, third, and fourth components that will be correlated with the complex wave are as shown in figure 10.23. All of them are, of course, multiples of 39 Hz.

Some of the higher-frequency components in the DFT are shown in figure 10.24. These higher frequencies are defined by fewer points per cycle. The highest frequency has one positive point and one negative point per cycle (it is not shown in figure 10.24, as it would appear as a solid black area on this scale).

We have noted that the highest frequency that could be present in the wave that we are analyzing, the Nyquist frequency, is 5,000 Hz. As each of the component frequencies is separated from the next by 39 Hz, the total number of possible frequency components is 5,000/39 =

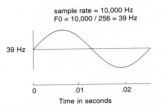

Fig. 10.22. The first wave that will be correlated in a DFT analysis with the part of the complex wave in the window in fig. 10.21.

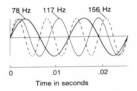

Fig. 10.23. The second, third, and fourth components that will be used in the DFT analysis.

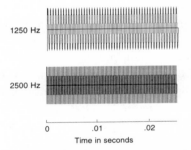

Fig. 10.24. Some of the higher-frequency components in the DFT.

128. This is half the window length, as is apparent when we summarize all these relations in the form of a set of statements for a computer program (in the Pascal language "**div**" is used to signify "divided by" when using integers):

NyquistFrequency := SampleRate **div** 2;
intervalBetweenComponents := SampleRate **div**
                                                            windowLength;
numberOfComponents := NyquistFrequency **div**
                                            intervalBetweenComponents;
{or}
numberOfComponents := (SampleRate **div** 2) **div**
                                (SampleRate **div** windowLength);

When calculating a DFT we have to determine the correlation between each of the possible components and
the portion of the wave in the window. Each correlation is
determined in the way shown above for the first component frequency. We calculate a sine wave and a cosine
wave corresponding to each frequency, determine the
cross products for each point, sum these, and then con-
vert this into a dB difference with respect to some arbitrary wave. These numbers constitute the spectrum of
the wave in terms of the relative amplitudes of the sinusoidal components.

As we have seen, the interval between consecutive
components depends on the fundamental frequency of
the wave in the window, which in turn depends on the
window length and the sampling rate. Very often the
sampling rate is fixed by the hardware used in the analog
to digital conversion, and we can manipulate only the
window length. If we want to have a smaller interval between components, we have to use a longer window. A
500-point window gives a frequency interval of 20 Hz (at
10,000 Hz sample rate), and a 1,000-point window would
give a frequency interval of 10 Hz. But although a window of 1,000 points would give more accurate frequency
resolution, it would have a duration of 100 ms, which
may be too long for the examination of rapidly changing
phenomena. If it is possible to vary the sample rate, then
we can get more accurate frequency determination with-

out lengthening the duration of the window. As we saw, the relation is: frequency interval = sample rate / number of points in the window. So we could get a smaller frequency interval by *lowering* the sample rate. The disadvantage here is that this would also lower the highest frequency that could be determined in the spectrum.

Table 10.5 illustrates these relationships. Which particular combination of sample rate and window length is most appropriate depends on the circumstances. When investigating long steady-state vowels, in which the higher frequencies are not relevant, it might be possible to use a 10,000 Hz sample rate and a window length of 1,024 points. When investigating stop bursts in which the higher frequencies are more important, a 20,000 Hz sample rate and a 128-point window might be the best choice.

Table 10.5 The Relation between the Sample Rate, the Window Length, and the Frequencies

Sample Rate	Window Duration		Interval between Components	Highest Frequency
(Hz)	(Points)	(Ms)	(Hz)	(Hz)
20,000	1024	51.2	19.53	10,000
	512	25.6	39.06	
	256	12.8	78.12	
	128	6.4	156.24	
10,000	1024	102.4	9.76	5,000
	512	51.2	19.53	
	256	25.6	39.06	
	128	12.8	78.12	
5,000	1024	204.8	4.88	2,500
	512	102.4	9.76	
	256	51.2	19.53	
	128	25.6	39.06	

Table 10.5 makes it evident that, for a given sample rate, if the frequency has to be determined more accurately, then more points are required in the window (and thus the time is known less accurately). For a given number of points in the window, if the frequency has to be determined more accurately, then a lower sample rate is required (and thus the highest frequency that can be determined is lower). The general principle is that you can't cheat Mother Nature.

The DFT (Discrete Fourier Transform) is a comparatively slow calculation on a computer. A similar calculation, known as a Fast Fourier Transform (FFT) is very much faster, but it can be used only with a window length that is a power of 2 (e.g., 64, 128, 256, or 1024 points). The necessity for the FFT window to be a power of 2 has colored speech technology and much speech research over the last twenty years.

Finally, we can sum up the material presented in this chapter and gain a more comprehensive understanding of the DFT by considering a slightly larger fragment of a program for this purpose shown below. We will assume that the wave has been sampled and read into an array of integer values, complexWave[n].

```
Program DFT;
Const
    SampleRate = 10000; { These two numbers would normally
                                be menu selectable, or}
    PointsInWindow = 256; { provided by some other part of the
                                total program. }
var
    numberOfFrequencyComponents, component, n: integer;
    radianFactor, sineAmplitude, cosAmplitude: real;
    complexWave: array[1..1000] of integer;
    componentAmplitude: array[1..128] of real;
```

```
begin
   numberOfFrequencyComponents := PointsInWindow div 2;
   for component := 1 to numberOfFrequencyComponents do
      {Calculate the correlation for each possible component fre-
      quency }
   begin
      {make a new "radianFactor" for each component}
      radianFactor := component * 2.0 * Pi/PointsInWindow;
      sineAmplitude := 0; { zero the variables }
      cosAmplitude := 0; { used for accumulating sums }
      for n := 1 to numberOfPoints do {calculate and sum the
                                       cross product for each point}
      begin
         sineAmplitude := complexWave[n] *
                           sin( n * radianFactor ) + sineAmplitude;
         cosAmplitude := complex Wave[n] *
                          cos( n * radianFactor )+ cosAmplitude;
      end;
{ express each component amplitude in dB = 10* log to base 10
of the power spectrum }
      componentAmplitude[component] := 10*
                  log10(sineAmplitude^2 + cosAmplitude ^2 );
   end;
end.
```

CHAPTER ELEVEN
Digital Filters and LPC Analysis

The Fourier transform is not the only way of determining the spectrum of a sound. A technique much in use in phonetic analysis involves determining what are called the Linear Predictor Coefficients of a sound wave. This procedure, known as LPC analysis, is a little more complex than Fourier analysis by a Discrete Fourier Transform (DFT), described in the previous chapter. However, it is possible to provide a simple overview of the underlying mathematical principles that assumes nothing about matrix algebra or complex numbers. But, be warned, it will require patient working through some cumbersome elementary equations.

As we saw in chapter 7, we can describe many of the sounds of speech in terms of a source-filter theory, summarized in figure 7.7, reproduced here as the top half of figure 11.1. We have added to the original figure 7.7, in that we have imagined that we began with a zero input which then became shaped so that it was equivalent to the vocal cord source, a set of pulses with a particular shape. Of course, if there really were a zero input and no generator within the system, there would be no output. The notion of a zero input is simply a convenient way of emphasizing that the vocal cord pulses are part of the

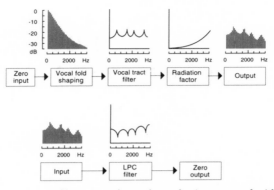

Fig. 11.1. A source-filter view of speech synthesis compared with LPC analysis.

production system. From there the diagram goes on as before, with the sound produced at the glottis being filtered by the vocal tract, and then becoming a source of sound radiating out from the lips. The sound wave that is produced is represented by its spectrum on the right at the top of figure 11.1.

The basic notion of an LPC analysis is shown in the lower part of the figure. It can be regarded as the reverse of the process of speech production. In this analysis scheme, the input is a speech wave (represented here by its spectrum), which is passed through a filter that is the inverse of this spectrum and that will produce as close to a zero output as possible. There is a major difference between the two systems, apart from the fact that one is an account of speech synthesis and the other a system for speech analysis. In the LPC approach the spectral shaping characteristics of the glottal source and of the lip radiation are incorporated into the same filter as that representing the characteristics of the vocal tract. Consequently the LPC filter is not exactly the same as the vocal tract filter. It does, however, have the same general shape; and the important similarity between the two systems is that in each case the principal activity is one of filtering a waveform. Accordingly, we will begin this account of LPC analysis by considering filters in digital terms.

Digital Filters

The characteristics of a filter are usually expressed in spectral terms. In chapters 5 and 6, when we first discussed filters, we did this by considering an input wave and then stating the center frequency and the bandwidth of the spectrum that the filter would pass. But in digital speech processing, it is not a wave that serves as input to the filter; it is a set of samples representing the amplitudes at discrete moments in time. We must therefore consider how the characteristics of a filter can be specified as an action performed on these points.

One example of such a specification is that for a moving average (MA) filter, which is a filter in which each point is replaced by the average of itself and the points around it. Consider the wave in figure 11.2(*a*). If this sound is transmitted through a noisy channel, such as a bad telephone line, it will have added random noise, as shown in figure 11.2(*b*). We can remove some of this noise by passing the wave through a filter that replaces every point by the mean of the point itself and a number of points on either side, thus taking a moving average. In this way we can recover something more like the original wave, although still with several irregularities, as shown in figure 11.2(*c*).

A more detailed look at this process is given in figure 11.3, which shows the individual points in a part of the noisy wave in figure 11.2(*b*), and the points after passing

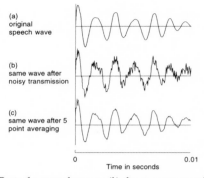

Fig. 11.2. (*a*) Part of a speech wave; (*b*) the same wave after it has been passed through a noisy transmission channel; (*c*) the noisy wave after it has been passed through a running average filter, so that each point has been replaced by the mean of the point itself and the two points before it and the two points after it.

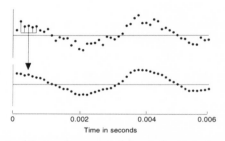

Fig. 11.3. Parts of the two lower waveforms in fig. 11.2, showing in more detail how each point in the smoothed wave is the mean of five points in the noisy wave.

them through a filter which replaces every point by the mean of that point and the two points before it and the two points after it. In this particular example we are considering sets of five points. Instead of a five-point moving average, we could have taken a larger or a smaller number of points into account, thus producing more or less smoothing of the input wave.

Obviously, to create a filter of this kind, we simply sum the amplitudes of the points, and then divide by the number of points in the sum. Put more formally, we can say that y_n, by which we mean the amplitude of the output y at a given time n, is the mean of the input x at time n and a number of earlier and later points, in our example, the two points before and the two points after time n. We can express this notion in terms of an equation giving the amplitude of any point y_n:

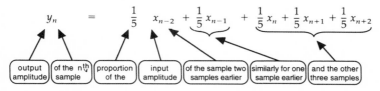

Without the additional commentary this equation is:

$$y_n = \frac{1}{5} x_{n-2} + \frac{1}{5} x_{n-1} + \frac{1}{5} x_n + \frac{1}{5} x_{n+1} + \frac{1}{5} x_{n+2}$$

In this filter, each point contributed equally to the moving average. But this is not the only way in which we can make the output a smoother form of the input. We could have decided that we wanted to make the output at a given time depend primarily on the amplitude of the point at that time, and less and less on the amplitudes of points further away. In other words, we could have added different weights to the points, instead of having them all 1/5. Our equation might have been:

$$y_n = \frac{1}{10} x_{n-2} + \frac{1}{5} x_{n-1} + \frac{2}{5} x_n + \frac{1}{5} x_{n+1} + \frac{1}{10} x_{n+2}.$$

Alternatively, we could also have considered a greater number of points and also had varying weights as in the following equation, in which the points before the point being considered are weighted more heavily than the points after it:

$$y_n = \frac{1}{3} x_{n-3} + \frac{1}{5} x_{n-2} + \frac{1}{7} x_{n-1} + \frac{1}{9} x_n + \frac{1}{12} x_{n+1}$$

$$+ \frac{1}{14} x_{n+2} + \frac{1}{16} x_{n+3}.$$

Note also that there is no reason for the weights given to each point to add up to one. Consider a filter in which:

$$y_n = 2x_{n-1} + 3x_n + 2x_{n+1}$$

All this implies is that the output is not only the weighted sum of certain of the input points but is also amplified, so that the mean output has a greater absolute value than the mean input. Note also that if we want to describe a filter in more general terms, we can write:

$$y_n = ax_{n-1} + bx_n + \ldots$$

where the a and b correspond to the weights in the previous equations.

A moving average filter of the kind we have specified is actually somewhat complicated in that the output at any moment depends on the input at both past and future moments. The output must be delayed somewhat with respect to the input in order to do these calculations. We will consider a simpler set of filters, the class of filters in which the output depends only on the current and past moments in time. The general specification for a digital filter considering only these moments in time is:

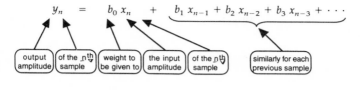

$$y_n = b_0 x_n + b_1 x_{n-1} + b_2 x_{n-2} + b_3 x_{n-3}, \ldots \qquad (1)$$

The weights (the values of the bs in the equation) are known as the coefficients of the filter. They are subscripted with reference to time $n = 0$, so the first coefficient is b_0, the second, which corresponds to time $n - 1$, is b_1, and so on. (We will use this correspondence in the numbering in our calculations later on.) If the filter involves attaching weights to N points, then we can say that it is an Nth-order filter.

What would be the values of y_n, the output of the filter, if the input consisted of a single pulse? Let us assume that this input pulse has an amplitude of one, and occurs at a time we will call time zero. Thus $x_n = 1$ when n is zero, but $x_n = 0$ when n has any value other than zero. This input is shown in table 11.1, and diagrammatically in figure 11.4.

Table 11.1 Specification of a Unit Pulse Input, a Set of Four Filter Coefficients, and the Output

Input		Filter		Output	
Sample Number	Amplitude	Coefficient Number	Value	Sample Number	Amplitude
x_{n-2}	0			y_{n-2}	0.0
x_{n-1}	0			y_{n-1}	0.0
x_n	1	b_0	0.5	y_n	0.5
x_{n+1}	0	b_1	−0.3	y_{n+1}	−0.3
x_{n+2}	0	b_2	0.2	y_{n+2}	0.2
x_{n+3}	0	b_3	−0.1	y_{n+3}	−0.1
x_{n+4}	0			y_{n+4}	0.0
x_{n+5}	0			y_{n+5}	0.0

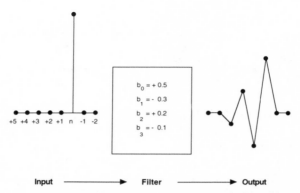

Fig. 11.4. An input, a filter, and its output as specified in table 11.1.

As we have noted, the bs in equation (1) denote the weights that have to be given to the input samples. They might have any values—this is a general equation. To make the discussion more concrete, we will consider a particular filter, one with four coefficients and the values (which are purely arbitrary) as shown. We can see what the output will be when we substitute values for b into equation (1), so that we get:

$$y_n = 0.5\,x_n - 0.3\,x_{n-1} + 0.2\,x_{n-2} - 0.1\,x_{n-3}.$$

Now consider what happens at various times, i.e., for different values of n. Obviously for values of n less than zero (that is, for all moments before the input impulse occurred), there will be no output, so y_n is zero. But consider what happens when $n = 0$ (i.e., at time zero, when the impulse occurred). Putting $n = 0$ in the equation, we have:

$$y_0 = 0.5x_0 - 0.3x_{-1} + 0.2x_{-2} - 0.1x_{-3}$$

We also know that $x_0 = 1$, $x_{-1} = 0$, $x_{-2} = 0$, $x_{-3} = 0$. Substituting these values in the equation we get:

$$y_0 = 0.5\,(1) - 0.3\,(0) + 0.2\,(0) - 0.1\,(0).$$
$$y_0 = 0.5.$$

Now consider the next sample, when $n = 1$. This time, so as to give a different view of the process, we will substitute the values for n into equation (1) before we substitute the values for b. This gives:

$$y_1 = b_0 x_1 + b_1 x_{1-1} + b_2 x_{1-2} + b_3 x_{1-3}$$
$$= b_0 x_1 + b_1 x_0 + b_2 x_{-1} + b_3 x_{-2}.$$

As before, $x_0 = 1$, and x_n for all other values of n is zero, so:

$$y_1 = b_0 0 + b_1 1 + b_2 0_0 + b_3 0$$
$$= b_1 = -0.3.$$

Similarly, we find that $y_2 = b_2 = 0.2$, and $y_3 = b_3 = -0.1$, which are the values shown in the graphical representation in figure 11.4.

The general equation (1) that we started with made the output of a filter dependent on the current input and all past inputs. We have now shown that when the input to a filter consists of a single impulse with an amplitude of one, the output samples will have values that correspond to the weights. This gives us one way of determining the frequency characteristics of a filter. We can put a pulse with an amplitude of one (a unit pulse) in, take the output wave (the impulse response, which is equivalent to the filter coefficients), and determine its frequency components. In the previous chapter we saw how to calculate a spectrum of a wave by using a Fourier analysis. All we need to do to determine the spectral characteristics of a digital filter is to calculate the Fourier transform of the filter coefficients. If we know the coefficients, we can calculate the spectrum. Unfortunately, however, it is not so simple to do this procedure in reverse, that is, knowing the spectrum of a filter, to calculate the coefficients.

LPC Analysis

As indicated in figure 11.1, Linear Predictive Coding (LPC) involves finding a filter that has a resonance curve which is the inverse of the spectrum of a given wave. As we have seen, digital filters can be defined in terms of a set of coefficients. It is also possible to use a set of coefficients to predict one point in a sampled wave from a knowledge of the values of a number of previous points (assuming that the wave is nonrandom and that it has regularities that can be predicted). The LPC algorithm makes a prediction of this kind by taking a number of previous points and multiplying each of them by a coefficient.

Consider a sampled wave such as that shown in figure 11.5. In general, if we want to predict the value of a particular point, we can do fairly well if we know the values of a sufficient number of the previous points. If we know twenty points, as in figure 11.6, we can make a good estimate of the value of the next point; but if we know only

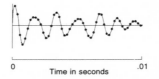

Fig. 11.5. A speech wave sampled at a number of points in time.

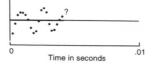

Fig. 11.6. Twenty points from a sampled wave allow the next point to be predicted with a reasonable accuracy.

Fig. 11.7. When only four points from a sampled wave are known it is difficult to predict the next point.

four points, as in figure 11.7, we can make only a rough guess.

The basic principle of the LPC algorithm is that any point can be regarded as simply the sum of a number of previous points, each of which has been multiplied by a suitable positive or negative number. The numbers used in the multiplications are called Linear Predictor Coefficients. We noted above that if we know the values of a sufficient number of the previous points in a sampled wave, we can make a good estimate of the value of the next point. In many cases it is true that the more points we know, the more accurately we can estimate the next point. But for some waves, if we know any two points, and we also know that it is a wave of a certain type, we can predict the values of all the other points. From our point of view, the important case of this kind is that of a damped sinusoidal wave. Figure 11.8 shows such a wave, with points at regular intervals represented by filled circles. Given the values of any two of these points,

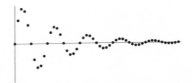

Fig. 11.8. A damped sinusoidal wave sampled at a number of points. Given the values of any two of these points we can predict the values of all succeeding points.

the value of the next point is fully determined. In other words, we can predict the value of the nth point, y_n, if we know the values of points y_{n-1} and y_{n-2}. The actual equation for the particular wave shown in figure 11.8 is:

$$y_n = 1.5\,y_{n-1} - 0.86\,y_{n-2}.$$

Table 11.2 shows the values of the first twenty points in figure 11.8, so that you can check this out for yourself. Note, for example, that the fourth point has a value of 43, which is 1.5 times the third point (1.5 * 76 = 114) plus −0.86 times the second point (−0.86 * 82 = −71, and 114 − 71 = 43). The same relationship is valid for all the points (subject to round-off errors in these integer numbers).

Speech analysis using an LPC approach relies on the fact that we can predict all the points in a damped sinusoidal wave from two coefficients. We saw in chapter 7 that a formant is simply a damped sinusoidal wave, and that many speech sounds are simply the sum of a number of formants repeated at intervals corresponding to pulses from the vocal cords. Roughly speaking, there is one formant per 1,000 Hz. (Remember that a neutral vowel has formants at about 500 Hz, 1,500 Hz, 2,500 Hz, 3,500 Hz, 4,500 Hz, etc.) If we are analyzing a speech wave that has

Table 11.2 The Values of the First Twenty Points in the Wave
Shown in Fig. 11.8

1	54	11	26
2	82	12	38
3	76	13	36
4	43	14	20
5	0	15	0
6	−37	16	−18
7	−56	17	−26
8	−52	18	−24
9	−30	19	−14
10	0	20	0

been sampled at 10,000 Hz and has frequencies up to
5,000 Hz, we can expect to find five formants. Each of
these can be considered as a damped sinusoid specified
by two coefficients, so we will need a filter with (at least)
ten coefficients. (We will actually need more, to account
for other factors that will be discussed later.)

In order to see how the process works, we will consider
a simplified case in which we analyze a wave in terms of
only four coefficients. We will analyze the wave represented by the sampled points in figure 11.9, considering
only the twelve points in the window. (Normally we
would consider a far larger window, as well as more coefficients.) The successive points in the window will be
designated by subscripts, s_1 through s_{12}. The particular
values for these points (on an arbitrary amplitude scale,
rounded off for plotting in the figure) are given in table
11.3.

We can predict s_5 from the four previous values, s_1, s_2,
s_3, s_4. We can do this by weighting (multiplying) each of
these four values by the appropriate LPC values, a_1, a_2,
a_3, a_4. Following a well-known statistical convention

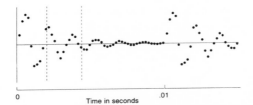

Fig. 11.9. A wave represented by sampled points. The twelve points in the window will be considered in an illustration of an LPC analysis.

Table 11.3 The Amplitudes of the Twelve Points in the Window in Fig. 11.9 (Rounded Off to Nearest Integer) and the Weighted Values of Previous Terms

n	Amplitude	$0.5*(n-1)$	$-0.6*(n-2)$	$0.4*(n-2)$	$-0.7*(n-4)$
1	90				
2	50	45.2			
3	17	25.3	−54.2		
4	−42	8.4	−30.3	36.1	
5	−74	−20.9	−10.1	20.2	−63.2
6	−40	−37.0	25.1	6.8	−35.4
7	−4	−20.3	44.4	−16.7	−11.8
8	22	−2.2	24.3	−29.6	29.2
9	49	10.9	2.6	−16.2	51.8
10	38	24.6	−13.1	−1.8	28.4
11	1	19.1	−29.5	8.7	3.1
12	−17	0.7	−22.9	19.6	−15.2

whereby a circumflex denotes an estimated value, we can call this estimated value $\hat{s}_5$, so that we can say:

$$\hat{s}_5 = a_1 s_4 + a_2 s_3 + a_3 s_2 + a_4 s_1. \tag{2}$$

The first term in the right-hand part of the equation simply says that we multiply the value for the point immediately before s_5 by some yet undetermined constant a_1, the term before that (i.e., s_3) by another constant a_2, and so on. In the example being considered, as we know the values for each of these points, we can say that:

$$\hat{s}_5 = -42\,a_1 + 17\,a_2 + 50\,a_3 + 90\,a_4. \tag{3}$$

In the general case of a point that we can call s_n, we can write:

$$\hat{s}_n = a_1\,s_{n-1} + a_2\,s_{n-2} + a_3\,s_{n-3} + a_4\,s_{n-4} \tag{4}$$

where a_1, a_2, a_3, a_4 are the LPC values, and s_{n-1}, s_{n-2}, s_{n-3}, s_{n-4} are the four preceding points, whose values are known.

To consider a few more specific cases, we would like to determine values for these coefficients a_1, a_2, a_3, a_4 that would predict equally well all the other points shown, so that it would be true that:

$$s\$_6 = a_1\,s_5 + a_2\,s_4 + a_3\,s_3 + a_4\,s_2 \tag{5}$$
$$= -74\,a_1 - 42\,a_2 + 17\,a_3 + 50\,a_4.$$
$$s\$_7 = a_1\,s_6 + a_2\,s_5 + a_3\,s_4 + a_4\,s_3$$
$$= -40\,a_1 - 74\,a_2 - 42\,a_3 + 17\,a_4.$$
$$s\$_8 = a_1\,s_7 + a_2\,s_6 + a_3\,s_5 + a_4\,s_4$$
$$= -4\,a_1 - 40\,a_2 - 74\,a_3 - 42\,a_4.$$
$$s\$_9 = a_1\,s_8 + a_2\,s_7 + a_3\,s_6 + a_4\,s_5$$
$$= 22\,a_1 - 4\,a_2 - 40\,a_3 - 74\,a_4.$$

If each point were correctly predicted, there would be no difference between it and its estimated value, and we could write for the general case:

$$0 = s_n - \hat{s}_n. \tag{6}$$

We know what $\hat{s}_n$ is from (3), so we can write:

$$0 = s_n - (a_1 s_{n-1} + a_2 s_{n-2} + a_3 s_{n-3} + a_4 s_{n-4}), \qquad (7)$$

where the parenthesized set of terms is exactly the same as the set of terms we used for estimating the value of s_n in (4) above. In the case of the particular points considered in (5), we have the following four sets of equations:

$$s\$_6 - s_6 = 0 \qquad\qquad\qquad\qquad\qquad\qquad (8)$$
$$= -40 - (-74\,a_1 - 42\,a_2 + 17\,a_3 + 50\,a_4).$$
$$s\$_7 - s_7 = 0$$
$$= -4 - (-74\,a_1 - 54\,a_2 + 16\,a_3 + 97\,a_4).$$
$$s\$_8 - s_8 = 0$$
$$= 22 - (-40\,a_1 - 79\,a_2 - 54\,a_3 + 16\,a_4).$$
$$s\$_9 - s_9 = 0$$
$$= 49 - (-4\,a_1 - 59\,a_2 - 79\,a_3 - 54\,a_4).$$

We now have four equations with four unknowns. We (or a computer program) could solve these four simultaneous equations and find the values of a_1, a_2, a_3, a_4 that would be appropriate for the five points s_5, s_6, s_7, s_8, s_9. It turns out that the answer is $a_1 = 0.5$, $a_2 = -0.6$, $a_3 = 0.4$, $a_4 = -0.7$. The last four columns in table 11.3 show the results of multiplying preceding points by these values, so that you can check this for yourself. (In these multiplications, additional decimal places have been included that are not included in the first column, which shows the numbers used in plotting the wave in fig. 11.9). For example, as indicated in the table:

$$s_6 - (\hat{s}\$_6) = 0 \quad -40 - (-74\,a_1 \quad \left| \quad -74.0* \quad 0.5 \quad = -37.0 \right.$$

$$-42\,a_2 \quad \left| \quad -41.8* \;\; -0.6 \quad = +25.1 \right.$$

$$+17\,a_3 \quad \left| \quad +16.9* \quad 0.4 \quad = \;\; +6.8 \right.$$

$$+50\,a_4) \quad \left| \quad +50.5* \;\; -0.7 \quad = -35.4 \right.$$

$$= \quad 40.5.$$

We want to have values for the LPC filter that would be appropriate not only for a particular set of four points but for any set of four points in the part of the wave being analyzed. Solving the equations in (8) gives us values of a_1, a_2, a_3, a_4 that are appropriate for points s_6, s_7, s_8, s_9, but they would give an error if used to estimate a fifth point from any other set of four points. The error for any point s_n, will be called e_n, where:

$$e_n = (\hat{s}_n - s_n)^2, \tag{9}$$

that is, the error is taken to be the square of the difference between the estimated and the known values. (Squared so that it makes a positive number, irrespective of whether $\hat{s}_n$ is greater or less than s_n.)

We are usually considering a window, a portion of a waveform consisting of a number of sampled points. In the window in figure 11.9 there are twelve points. There are thus eight sets of four points that can be used to estimate a fifth, each with some error, as exemplified by equations (10). (At this point you should be looking at blocks of equations as a whole. Look at the first line and see that you can understand it; then scan down the columns to see how each line differs from the line above it.)

$$e_5 = (\hat{s}_5 - s_5)^2 \tag{10}$$

$$= (a_1 s_4 + a_2 s_3 + a_3 s_2 + a_4 s_1 - s_5)^2.$$

$$e_6 = (\hat{s}_6 - s_6)^2$$

$$= (a_1 s_5 + a_2 s_4 + a_3 s_3 + a_4 s_2 - s_6)^2.$$

$$e_7 = (\hat{s}_7 - s_7)^2$$

$$= (a_1 s_6 + a_2 s_5 + a_3 s_4 + a_4 s_3 - s_7)^2.$$

$$e_8 = (\hat{s}_8 - s_8)^2$$

$$= (a_1 s_7 + a_2 s_6 + a_3 s_5 + a_4 s_4 - s_8)^2.$$

$$e_9 = (\hat{s}_9 - s_9)^2$$

$$= (a_1 s_8 + a_2 s_7 + s_3 s_6 + a_4 s_5 - s_9)^2.$$

$$e_{10} = (\hat{s}_{10} - s_{10})^2$$

$$= (a_1 s_9 + a_2 s_8 + a_3 s_7 + a_4 s_6 - s_{10})^2.$$

$$e_{11} = (\hat{s}_{11} - s_{11})^2$$

$$= (a_1 s_{10} + a_2 s_9 + a_3 s_8 + a_4 s_7 - s_{11})^2.$$

$$e_{12} = (\hat{s}_{12} - s_{12})^2$$

$$= (a_1 s_{11} + a_2 s_{10} + a_3 s_9 + a_4 s_8 - s_{12})^2.$$

The LPC algorithm solves the sets of simultaneous equations for the points in the window while trying to minimize the sum of these error terms. The problem is to find values of the coefficients such that each contributes as little as possible to the total error in the window. As we will see, the process of finding the appropriate LPC values is fairly lengthy, but it is worth doing (or more precisely, letting a computer do it) because the coefficients have some very useful properties. Firstly, they are an efficient way of describing a speech sound in terms of a small set of numbers; the LPC values can be used to reconstruct the original waveform with a fair degree of precision. Secondly, and more importantly to phoneticians who are not often concerned with efficient methods of storing representations of speech waveforms, LPC values can themselves be analyzed to provide estimates of the formant frequencies.

The mathematics involved in solving the LPC equations is a little cumbersome but not very complicated. Apart from one small piece of high school algebra (differentiating an expression, which will be fully exemplified), it involves only basic arithmetic operations. In the following section we will go through the process in a considerable amount of detail. The mathematically more sophisticated reader may wish to move directly to the next section, where we will recapitulate the process using conventional mathematical abbreviations. If you do not wish to know exactly how the LPC equations work, you can skip to the final section, where we will consider the use of LPCs in speech analysis.

We will begin by considering the general form for the error for any point in a window (still presuming we are using only four points as predictors of the next point):

$$e_n = (a_1 s_{n-1} + a_2 s_{n-2} + a_3 s_{n-3} + a_4 s_{n-4} - s_n)^2. \quad (11)$$

The terms in this equation can be rearranged as in (12), in which the final $-s_n$ is moved to the start of the right-hand side:

$$e_n = (-s_n + a_1 s_{n-1} + a_2 s_{n-2} + a_3 s_{n-3} + a_4 s_{n-4})^2. \quad (12)$$

Putting $-s_n$ as the first term allows us to see how we can further simplify the expression. If we multiply s_n by a constant, a_0, which we set at -1, it will have no effect other than letting us get rid of the minus sign, so that we can rewrite (12) as:

$$e_n = (a_0 s_n + a_1 s_{n-1} + a_2 s_{n-2} + a_3 s_{n-3} + a_4 s_{n-4})^2 \qquad (13)$$
where $a_0 = -1$.

In terms of the estimate of the value of a particular point, this would be:

$$e_5 = (a_0 s_5 + a_1 s_4 + a_2 s_3 + a_3 s_2 + a_4 s_1)^2. \qquad (14)$$

In this way we can make all the terms look more alike, which is an important consideration when we come to set up a computer program in which the same operations can be repeated over and over again. Next, in order to multiply out the parenthesized term on the right (i.e., to do the squaring) we have to multiply each term by all the others, so that we get the following equation (again look at the first line and then compare terms in this line with those in the lines below):

$$(15)$$

$$
\begin{aligned}
e_n = {} & a_0 s_n a_0 s_n && + a_0 s_n a_1 s_{n-1} && + a_0 s_n a_2 s_{n-2} && + a_0 s_n a_3 s_{n-3} && + a_0 s_n a_4 s_{n-4} \\
& + a_1 s_{n-1} a_0 s_n && + a_1 s_{n-1} a_1 s_{n-1} && + a_1 s_{n-1} a_2 s_{n-2} && + a_1 s_{n-1} a_3 s_{n-3} && + a_1 s_{n-1} a_4 s_{n-4} \\
& + a_2 s_{n-2} a_0 s_n && + a_2 s_{n-2} a_1 s_{n-1} && + a_2 s_{n-2} a_2 s_{n-2} && + a_2 s_{n-2} a_3 s_{n-3} && + a_2 s_{n-2} a_4 s_{n-4} \\
& + a_3 s_{n-3} a_0 s_n && + a_3 s_{n-3} a_1 s_{n-1} && + a_3 s_{n-3} a_2 s_{n-2} && + a_3 s_{n-3} a_3 s_{n-3} && + a_3 s_{n-3} a_4 s_{n-4} \\
& + a_4 s_{n-4} a_0 s_n && + a_4 s_{n-4} a_1 s_{n-1} && + a_4 s_{n-4} a_2 s_{n-2} && + a_4 s_{n-4} a_3 s_{n-3} && + a_4 s_{n-4} a_4 s_{n-4}.
\end{aligned}
$$

Or if you prefer to look at the expanded form for a particular point, say s_5, we can exemplify (15) as:

$$(16)$$

$$e_5 = a_0s_5\,a_0s_5 + a_0s_5\,a_1s_4 + a_0s_5\,a_2s_3 + a_0s_5\,a_3s_2 + a_0s_5\,a_4s_1$$

$$+ a_1s_4\,a_0s_5 + a_1s_4\,a_1s_4 + a_1s_4\,a_2s_3 + a_1s_4\,a_3s_2 + a_1s_4\,a_4s_1$$

$$+ a_2s_3\,a_0s_5 + a_2s_3\,a_1s_4 + a_2s_3\,a_2s_3 + a_2s_3\,a_3s_2 + a_2s_3\,a_4s_1$$

$$+ a_3s_2\,a_0s_5 + a_3s_2\,a_1s_4 + a_3s_2\,a_2s_3 + a_3s_2\,a_3s_2 + a_3s_2\,a_4s_1$$

$$+ a_4s_1\,a_0s_5 + a_4s_1\,a_1s_4 + a_4s_1\,a_2s_3 + a_4s_1\,a_3s_2 + a_4s_1\,a_4s_1.$$

It is worth going through these equations carefully, noting that the order of the terms in a multiplication is irrelevant, so that we can rewrite $a_0s_5\,a_0s_5$, for example, as a_0a_0 s_5s_5 or $a_0^2\,s_5^2$. When we do this, we can see that the terms representing the squares of each of the original terms such as $(a_0\,s_n)\,(a_0\,s_n)$ are on the diagonal, as shown in figure 11.10. Note also that every term in the top right part of the matrix is paired with one in the lower left part (only some of the pairings are shown in fig. 11.10).

Now we want to look at the error not just for a single

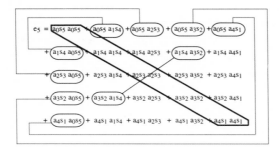

Fig. 11.10. Part of the matrix of terms used in an LPC equation, arranged as in (26) but showing squared terms on the diagonal. Some terms containing the same items in a different order are shown by linked lines.

point but for each of the points in the window. Putting n = 1, 2, . . . 8 in equation (15), we can get an equation for the total error in the window, which we will call E_w. This equation is a summation of the error terms in (10) above, but using a_0 as explained in (13).

$$E_w = (a_0s_5 + a_1s_4 + a_2s_3 + a_3s_2 + a_4s_1)^2 \quad (18)$$
$$+ (a_0s_6 + a_1s_5 + a_2s_4 + a_3s_3 + a_4s_2)^2$$
$$+ (a_0s_7 + a_1s_6 + a_2s_5 + a_3s_4 + a_4s_3)^2$$
$$+ (a_0s_8 + a_1s_7 + a_2s_6 + a_3s_5 + a_4s_4)^2$$
$$+ (a_0s_9 + a_1s_8 + a_2s_7 + a_3s_6 + a_4s_5)^2$$
$$+ (a_0s_{10} + a_1s_9 + a_2s_8 + a_3s_7 + a_4s_6)^2$$
$$+ (a_0s_{11} + a_1s_{10} + a_2s_9 + a_3s_8 + a_4s_7)^2$$
$$+ (a_0s_{12} + a_1s_{11} + a_2s_{10} + a_3s_9 + a_4s_8)^2$$

Expanding this out by squaring each of the lines in (18), we get a block of five lines corresponding to each line in (18). This is a rather horrendous expression, but by looking at the first line in each block, then at the block as a whole, and finally comparing the blocks, you should be able to see how it is organized. The first block is the same as in (16):

$$e_w = a_0s_5a_0s_5 + a_0s_5a_1s_4 + a_0s_5a_2s_3 + a_0s_5a_3s_2 + a_0s_5a_4s_1 \quad (19)$$
$$+ a_1s_4a_0s_5 + a_1s_4a_1s_4 + a_1s_4a_2s_3 + a_1s_4a_3s_2 + a_1s_4a_4s_1$$

$+ a_2s_3a_0s_5 + a_2s_3a_1s_4 + a_2s_3a_2s_3 + a_2s_3a_3s_2 + a_2s_3a_4s_1$

$+ a_3s_2a_0s_5 + a_3s_2a_1s_4 + a_3s_2a_2s_3 + a_3s_2a_3s_2 + a_3s_2a_4s_1$

$+ a_4s_1a_0s_5 + a_4s_1a_1s_4 + a_4s_1a_2s_3 + a_4s_1a_3s_2 + a_4s_1a_4s_1$

$+ a_0s_6a_0s_6 + a_0s_6a_1s_5 + a_0s_6a_2s_4 + a_0s_6a_3s_3 + a_0s_6a_4s_2$

$+ a_1s_5a_0s_6 + a_1s_5a_1s_5 + a_1s_5a_2s_4 + a_1s_5a_3s_3 + a_1s_5a_4s_2$

$+ a_2s_4a_0s_6 + a_2s_4a_1s_5 + a_2s_4a_2s_4 + a_2s_4a_3s_3 + a_2s_4a_4s_2$

$+ a_3s_3a_0s_6 + a_3s_3a_1s_5 + a_3s_3a_2s_4 + a_3s_3a_3s_3 + a_3s_3a_4s_4$

$+ a_4s_2a_0s_6 + a_4s_2a_1s_5 + a_4s_2a_2s_4 + a_4s_2a_3s_3 + a_4s_2a_4s_2$

$+ \text{etc: to}$

$+ a_0s_{12}a_0s_{12} + a_0s_{12}a_1s_{11} + a_0s_{12}a_2s_{10} + a_0s_{12}a_3s_9 + a_0s_{12}a_4s_8$

$+ a_1s_{11}a_0s_{12} + a_1s_{11}a_1s_{11} + a_1s_{11}a_2s_{10} + a_1s_{11}a_3s_9 + a_1s_{11}a_4s_8$

$+ a_2s_{10}a_0s_{12} + a_2s_{10}a_1s_{11} + a_2s_{10}a_2s_{10} + a_2s_{10}a_3s_9 + a_2s_{10}a_4s_8$

$+ a_3s_9a_0s_{12} + a_3s_9a_1s_{11} + a_3s_9a_2s_{10} + a_3s_9a_3s_9 + a_3s_9a_4s_8$

$+ a_4s_8a_0s_{12} + a_4s_8a_1s_{11} + a_4s_8a_2s_{10} + a_4s_8a_3s_9 + a_4s_8a_4s_8.$

Our problem is to make each of the terms a_1, a_2, a_3, a_4 contribute as little as possible to the error. The next step is to rearrange the order of the sums so as to gather together all the terms containing a_1, all those containing a_2, etc. (We do not need to do anything further about a_0 as we know it is -1). The set of terms for a_1 are as shown in figure 11.11. Note that there are eight terms of the form a_1^2 s_n^2 (e.g., $a_1 a_1 s_5 s_5$, and $a_1 a_1 s_6 s_6$, etc.), one in each of the submatrices. We can take all these terms together and write them as:

$$a_1^2 (s_5^2 + s_6^2 + s_7^2 + s_8^2 + s_9^2 + s_{10}^2 + s_{11}^2 + s_{12}^2). \quad (20)$$

We know the values of all the s terms, so we can write this as a_1^2 (knownValues). In the case of the wave shown in figure 11.9 and the values in table 11.3:

$$s_5^2 + s_6^2 + s_7^2 + s_8^2 + s_9^2 + s_{10}^2 + s_{11}^2 + s_{12}^2$$
$$= 74*74 + 40*40 + 4*4 + 22*22 + 49*49 + 38*38 + 1*1$$
$$+ 17*17$$
$$= 11,711.$$

Similarly, each of the terms containing a_2^2, a_3^2, a_4^2 can be written as a_2^2(knownValues), a_3^2(knownValues), a_4^2(knownValues).

Fig. 11.11. All the terms containing the variable a_1 in the LPC matrix are enclosed. The terms containing a_1^2 are further enclosed within ovals.

Still considering just terms containing a_1, we can see that there are also two examples of each of the other terms in the pattern, linked as shown in figure 11.11. These can be summed as:

$$2a_1a_0(s_4s_5 + s_5s_6 + s_6s_7 + s_7s_8 + s_8s_9 + s_9s_{10} + s_{10}s_{11} + s_{11}s_{12}) \quad (21)$$

$$+ \ 2a_1a_2(s_4s_5 + s_5s_6 + s_6s_7 + s_7s_8 + s_8s_9 + s_9s_{10} + s_{10}s_{11} + s_{11}s_{12})$$

$$+ \ 2a_1a_3(s_4s_5 + s_5s_6 + s_6s_7 + s_7s_8 + s_8s_9 + s_9s_{10} + s_{10}s_{11} + s_{11}s_{12})$$

$$+ \ 2a_1a_4(s_4s_5 + s_5s_6 + s_6s_7 + s_7s_8 + s_8s_9 + s_9s_{10} + s_{10}s_{11} + s_{11}s_{12}).$$

In the case of the wave shown in figure 11.9 and the values in table 11.3, the values:

$$s_4\, s_5 + s_5\, s_6 + s_6\, s_7 + s_7\, s_8 + s_8\, s_9 + s_9\, s_{10} + s_{10}\, s_{11} + s_{11}\, s_{12}$$
are:

$$(-42 * -74) + (-74 * -40) + (-40 * -4) + (-4 * 22) +$$
$$(22 * 49) + (49 * 38) + (38 * 1) + (1 * -17),$$

which comes to 9,101. Accordingly, noting that $2 * 9,101 = 18,202$, and remembering that a_0 was set to -1, we can rewrite the terms in (21) as:

$$- \ 2\, a_1 + 18{,}202\, a_1\, a_2 + 18{,}202\, a_1\, a_3 + 18{,}202\, a_1\, a_4. \quad (22)$$

As we noted earlier, we want to find a value of a_1 such that it contributes as little as possible to the total error. This error depends directly on the terms in (20) and (21). In the particular case we are considering, these two terms can be added together, so that we can write:

$$\text{error } a_1 = 11{,}711\, a_1{}^2 - 2\, a_1 + 18{,}202\, a_1\, a_2 + 18{,}202\, a_1\, a_3$$
$$+ \ 18{,}202\, a_1\, a_4. \quad (23)$$

Expressed like this, these terms have the general form of a quadratic equation:

$$y = m\,x^2 + n\,x. \tag{24}$$

Functions of this kind have the form shown in figure 11.12, which illustrates three quadratic equations.

All quadratic equations—(23) as well as (24)—will have this general shape. As you can see from the graphs, this means that there is always some value of x (or in the case we have been considering, a_1) such that when we make a small change in its value, y (or error a_1) stops decreasing and starts increasing. This is the value that we want to find.

The minimum values for the equations in figure 11.12 are shown in the following table. This table also contains a column indicating how the minimum value for x can be found by the process known as differentiating, which shows the slope of the curve. When the slope of the curve is 0, it is flat. The general form for differentiating a quadratic equation of this kind is shown in the last row of the table.

Equation	Differentiate and Set to Zero	Minimum Value of X	Minimum Value of Y
$y = x^2 + 4x$	$2x + 4 = 0$	$x = -2$	$y = -4$
$y = x^2 - 4x$	$2x - 4 = 0$	$x = 2$	$y = -4$
$y = x^2 - 6x$	$2x - 6 = 0$	$x = 3$	$y = -9$
$y = x^2 + kx$	$2x + k = 0$	$x = -(k/2)$	$y = -(k^2/4)$

We can now see how we can determine the minimum value for a that applies to this set of twelve points. In order to find the minimum for the error curve (the point where the slope of this curve is zero), we differentiate the expression in (23) and set it to zero. We then get:

$$0 = 23{,}422\,a_1 - 2 + 18{,}202\,a_2 + 18{,}202\,a_3 + 18{,}202\,a_4. \tag{25}$$

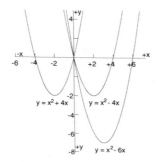

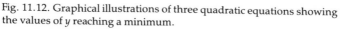

Fig. 11.12. Graphical illustrations of three quadratic equations showing the values of y reaching a minimum.

We can also form similar equations for the minimum error attributable to each of a_2, a_3, and a_4. This will give us a total of four equations with four unknowns, a_1, a_2, a_3, a_4, which can be solved simultaneously by simple algebra. As we have seen, using a computer to do all this complex shuffling of terms, it turns out that $a_1 = 0.5$, $a_2 = -0.6$, $a_3 = 0.4$, $a_4 = -0.7$. In the next section we will present a general version of this procedure. The final section will show how this can be used in speech analysis.

LPC Overview

We have demonstrated a procedure for taking a window consisting of a certain number of points (twelve in the case we have been discussing, but the same procedure would work for any number), taking subsets of these points (four in our case), and determining with minimum error the value of the next point in the window by multiplying each point in the subset by a coefficient. The procedure specifies a filter which, given an input consisting of a speech wave, will produce a minimum output.

Engineers and others with more mathematical training usually describe LPC analysis in somewhat different terms, as we will now do. The core of the procedure is to predict the amplitude of the nth sample in a signal, s_n. We do this by considering the sum of the p preceding points, $s_{n-1}, s_{n-2}, \cdots s_{n-p}$, each of which will be multiplied by a coefficient a_k, where k varies from 1 to p. Calling our prediction $\hat{s}_n$, and using the summation symbol Σ to indicate the sum of all the terms, we can write:

$$\hat{s}_n = \sum_{k=1}^{p} a_k s_{n-k}. \tag{26}$$

In words, this equation says that the estimated value of the amplitude of point s_n is equal to the sum of the p previous points, each of the previous points s_{n-k} being multiplied by a particular weight a_k. This is equivalent to (4) in the previous exposition. The difference between the prediction and the actual value represents the error, and, as before, we will call the square of this difference the error, e_n, as we did in (9):

$$e_n = (\hat{s}_n - s_n)^2. \tag{27}$$

Taking the value of $\hat{s}_n$ derived in (26) and substituting it in (27), we have:

$$e_n = \left(\sum_{k=1}^{p} a_k s_{n-k} - s_n \right)^2. \tag{28}$$

We are looking at the errors for each of the points in a window, which we will say is w points long. As we need p points in making each prediction, we will be calculating the errors for $(w - p)$ points. We will let E denote the sum of all the error terms e_n (where n varies from 1 to $w - p$). We can then write:

$$E = \sum_{n=1}^{w-p} e_n. \tag{29}$$

Stated in words, the total error, E, is the sum of the individual errors, e_n. Noting the value of e_n in (28), we can expand (29) into:

$$E = \sum_{n=1}^{w-p} \left(\sum_{k=1}^{p} a_k s_{n-k} - s_n \right)^2. \tag{30}$$

E can be minimized by a partial differentiation with respect to each of the coefficients, a_i setting:

$$\frac{\partial E}{\partial a_i} = 0. \qquad 1 \le i \le p. \tag{31}$$

This enables us to get the set of equations:

$$\sum_{k=1}^{p} a_k \sum_{n=1}^{w-p} s_{n-k} - s_{n-i} = \sum_{n=1}^{w-p} s_n - s_{n-1}. \tag{32}$$

$$1 \le i \le p.$$

Equation (32) is a set of p equations in p unknowns which can be solved for the predictor coefficients $\{a_k, 1 \le i \le p\}$ which minimize E in (30).

Interpreting LPCs

Our next task is to see how we can derive information from an LPC analysis. The most direct approach is to regard the coefficients as specifying a filter of the general form:

$$y_n = b_0 x_n + b_1 x_{n-1} + b_2 x_{n-2} + b_3 x_{n-3}, \ldots \qquad (1)$$

which is the equation we have been using in calculating the LPC. We saw at the beginning of this chapter what happens when the input to such a filter consists of a single impulse. The output wave is specified by the coefficients. Knowing the shape of the output wave, we can calculate the spectrum. In other words, putting in an impulse, which is equivalent to putting in an infinite number of components with an equal amplitude, we can observe the relative amplitudes of the components in the output and thus determine the spectrum of the filter. All we have to do in order to determine the spectrum is to regard LPC values as specifying a filter. We can then put a unit impulse into the filter and make a Fourier analysis of the output wave.

In the previous chapter we saw that the number of frequency components determined by a Fourier analysis depends on the sample rate (which we will regard as fixed in this discussion) and the number of samples in the FFT window. If we have a large number of points, we will have a large number of components within the frequency range defined by the sample rate. (Recall that with a 10,000 Hz sample rate defining a 5,000 Hz frequency range, if the window length is 256 points, there will be 128 frequency components at intervals of 39 Hz, but if the window length is 512 points, there will be 256 frequency components at intervals of 19 Hz.) As we will see, a typical LPC analysis has twelve or fourteen coefficients. We are regarding these coefficients as specifying an impulse response that decays to zero, so we can add as many zeros as we like to this "wave" before doing the FFT. If we pad the FFT with sufficient zeros at the end, we will be able to get a spectrum with a large number of components, so that we will have a smooth curve representing the response of the LPC filter.

At this point we should remember that an LPC filter lumps together several aspects of speech production, as we saw in figure 11.1. An LPC spectrum represents not only the formant frequencies due to the resonances of the vocal tract but also the effects of the lip radiation and the spectrum of the pulse from the vocal folds. Nevertheless, the peaks in the LPC spectrum are usually good indicators of the formant frequencies. Problems may arise when two formants are close together, in which case the spectrum may appear to have only a single peak corresponding to both of them, or when one formant has a lower amplitude, so that it appears as only a kink in the curve representing another formant. These problems lead us to another way of considering LPC analysis.

It is also possible to analyze an LPC expression so as to determine the exact frequencies corresponding to the poles (which, however, may not be exactly those of the formants in the vocal tract transfer function). For every pair of LPC terms we get a pair of numbers corresponding to the frequency and the bandwidth of a pole in the filter. We know from the discussion in chapter 10 that there will be a formant at 500 Hz, 1,500 Hz, 2,500 Hz, and so on in a neutral vowel for a speaker with a vocal tract of 17.5 cm. In general, for such a speaker there will be one formant for every 1,000 Hz interval. So with a 10,000 Hz sample rate and an upper frequency limit of 5,000 Hz, we can expect to find five formants. This will require ten LPC terms. If we want to allow two further terms to account for higher formants that may be influencing the spectrum or a pole due to the glottal pulse shape, then we should make a twelve-point LPC analysis. If the speaker might have a shorter vocal tract so that we could only expect four formants below 10,000 Hz, then we could use a ten-point LPC.

Choosing the right number of coefficients for an LPC analysis is somewhat of an art. If one chooses too many, the analysis will produce poles corresponding to spurious formants; if one chooses too few, formants may be lumped together because the higher formants or the glottal pulse may require more complex specification. The problem is compounded by the fact that an LPC analysis is equivalent to trying to model the spectrum using only poles, and there may be zeros (antiresonances) in the vocal tract transfer function. There certainly will be antiresonances in any vocal tract shape that contains the equivalent of a side tube, such as the oral cavity in the case of a nasal sound. LPC analysis is not reliable for nasalized vowels. A general rule of thumb for the number of coefficients is the sample rate in kHz plus 2, e.g., 10,000 Hz = 10 kHz plus 2 equals 12. But a better rule is to use several different analyses with different numbers of coefficients and see which gives the most interpretable results.

As a final point we should consider the error term in the LPC output. We noted earlier that if we took a single set of p points, we could find a set of p coefficients that could be used to specify the exact value of the next point. The problem came when we wanted to use these same p coefficients to specify the next point for a different set of points in the window. The LPC process finds the best set of coefficients that minimizes the error for each set of points in a window. In these circumstances, each determination will have some error; and the error will be greatest when there is a large change in the part of the wave within the window. Figure 11.13 makes this clear by showing the error associated with the prediction of each point when using fourteen coefficients in an LPC procedure applied to an actual speech wave. This error is known as the LPC residual.

The error is at a maximum around those points that occur when the wave changes abruptly due to the impulses from the vibrations of the vocal folds. As a result, the LPC residual provides a good way of determining the pitch of a signal. We can take the LPC residual and compute the autocorrelation function, as we did in chapter 9; but this time we will find that there is only one large peak in the autocorrelation function, and this peak corresponds to the interval between vocal cord pulses. In the case of LPC analysis, even the errors are useful.

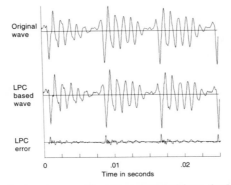

Fig. 11.13. An input wave, the wave calculated from the LPC, and the LPC residual, the difference between these two waves. The equation used for calculating each point is: $y_n = -1.87554 * y_{n-1} + 1.27243 * y_{n-2} - 0.18456 * y_{n-3} - 0.18403 * y_{n-4} + 0.06146 * y_{n-5} + 0.01238 * y_{n-6} + 0.04827 * y_{n-7} - 0.01642 * y_{n-8} - 0.04343 * y_{n-9} + 0.05991 * y_{n-10} + 0.06162 * y_{n-11} + 0.06531 * y_{n-12} - 0.12318 * y_{n-13} - 0.01060 * y_{n-14}.$

LPC, FFT, and autocorrelation functions are only a few of the procedures that are useful in speech analysis. Most of these procedures involve functions that are no more complex than those explained here. Furthermore, nearly all of the acoustic differences between speech sounds can be described in terms of the general principles outlined in this book. Knowledge of these principles and familiarity with the computer techniques that have been outlined above will enable the reader to appreciate many of the problems that are being discussed in contemporary papers on acoustic phonetics.

INDEX